Lecture Notes in Computer Science 12030

More information about this series at http://www.springer.com/series/7410

Mattia Salnitri · Jan Jürjens ·
Haralambos Mouratidis ·
Loredana Mancini · Paolo Giorgini (Eds.)

Visual Privacy Management

Design and Applications of a Privacy-Enabling Platform

 Springer

Editors
Mattia Salnitri 🄳
Politecnico di Milano
Milan, Italy

Haralambos Mouratidis 🄳
University of Brighton
Brighton, UK

Paolo Giorgini 🄳
Department of Information Engineering
and Computer Science
University of Trento
Trento, Italy

Jan Jürjens 🄳
Institute for Software Technology IST
University of Koblenz-Landau
Koblenz, Germany

Fraunhofer ISST
Dortmund, Germany

Loredana Mancini 🄳
Axians Italia
Rome, Italy

ISSN 0302-9743   ISSN 1611-3349   (electronic)
Lecture Notes in Computer Science
ISBN 978-3-030-59943-0   ISBN 978-3-030-59944-7   (eBook)
https://doi.org/10.1007/978-3-030-59944-7

LNCS Sublibrary: SL4 – Security and Cryptology

This Springer imprint is published by the registered company Springer Nature Switzerland AG
The registered company address is: Gewerbestrasse 11, 6330 Cham, Switzerland

Preface

Recent privacy scandals, such as Cambridge Analytica in 2018 or the Swedish data leakage in 2017, and the creation and enforcement of the new General Data Protection Regulation (GDPR) in Europe in 2018, have captured the attention of any entity that operates with data.

The GDPR identifies European citizens as main stakeholders to be protected, creating powerful tools such as the consent mechanism and the right to be forgotten. Therefore, any organization that uses data of European citizens must adhere to the GDPR, otherwise heavy fines will be applied: up to 20 million euros, or 4% of the firm's worldwide annual revenue from the preceding financial year, whichever amount is higher.

Private companies have already started to take actions in order to be compliant with the GDPR. But privacy is not only a concern for companies, Public Administrations (PAs), that constantly use data of citizens, must protect citizens' data as well. Furthermore, dissimilar from private companies, citizens frequently have no option but to give their data to PAs in order to use essential public services. It is, therefore, a top priority for such organizations to give the feeling of protection and control of citizens' data.

Unfortunately, enforcing privacy requirements in PAs is no trivial task: PAs' information systems are usually extremely complex, with legacy pieces of software that were developed when privacy was not a concern at all. Moreover, PA is a heterogeneous category that covers organizations with very different objectives, users, and market segment. Examples of PAs are hospitals, government bodies, and public companies; all of them with complex information systems that manage data of large quantities of citizens.

The urgent need of public organizations is, therefore, to address privacy concerns being compliant with the GDPR and, in the meantime, to give the citizens the control of their data allowing them to specify privacy requirements.

This book describes the outcome of a project called VisiOn, that lasted three years, and where four universities and seven companies collaborated to create a platform that can be used by PAs to design or to adapt their information following privacy laws and privacy requirements of citizens. We called it VisiOn Privacy Platform (VPP). The book is the result of the collective effort of all project participants that contributed to the success of VisiOn. Project participants acted as reviewers for book chapters, and each chapter was reviewed by at least two reviewers.

The objective of this book is to provide readers a useful reference for the creation and validation of a software platform that enforces privacy in complex organizations such as PAs. This book is structured following the software engineering approach to the design of a complex software such as the VPP.

Chapter 1 defines the conceptual framework we created to define privacy concepts. This chapter gives shape to privacy principles using European Union laws as a starting point. Moreover, the chapter describes the principle on which we based most of the platform, i.e., privacy by design and a type of agreement we created to specify a privacy contract between a citizen and the PA, called Privacy Level Agreement (PLA).

Following that, in Chapter 2, requirements of the VPP are defined along with a method that we created and used for the elicitation, classification, prioritization, and validation of requirements for the VPP.

Chapter 3 describes the software components that were developed for the platform, and compose the VPP and external software tools that were developed by the partners for the VisiOn project, and that we integrated into the platform in order to use their functionalities. In particular, the chapter describes the architecture of the components and how their functionalities are offered and used in the VPP.

Chapter 4 focuses on the security and privacy analyses that can be executed using the VPP. It describes the two frameworks that compose the VPP, i.e., the desktop and the web framework. The former, dedicated to PA employees, that is used to perform privacy analyses, while the latter, dedicated mainly to the end users, i.e., the citizens, is used to elicit their privacy requirements and show them information about their sensitive data and how it is being used.

Chapter 5 describes the validation of the platform using three real case studies: two hospitals, a government body, and a public company. In each case study the VPP has been integrated in real information systems, facing very pragmatic issues, such as the integration with the authentication system of the organization in charge of the case study. After the integration, the VPP was used by PA employees (the Desktop Framework) and by citizens (the Web Framework) in order to collect feedback and evaluate the platform.

Each chapter of this book covers a part of the development and evaluation of VPP. Each of the chapters have two main contributions: one related to the platform, that delivers details on the platform, and one related to the abstract contribution that can be applied to other platforms as well. We believe that both contributions will help readers in other projects and research work.

A number of innovative technical solutions have been proposed in this book; the interested readers are invited to read cited publications and technical reports for more details of specific aspects. In the present book, the emphasis is on the presentation of the global approach developed in the project.

VPP sets the basis for an easier compliance of PA with GDPR and derived laws, while allowing citizens (users) to specify their privacy requirements, building their trust in the PAs they granted access to their sensitive data. However, we identified two main critical points that may weaken VPP positive impacts if not properly addressed when the platform is applied.

The first critical point concerns the ambiguity of the GDPR: some of the concepts and the constraints defined in this regulation are ambiguous. This is because the GDPR is enforced with laws defined by local privacy authorities of each member state of the European Union (EU). We created the VPP in order to adapt to such local laws. Therefore, VPP is not an off-the-shelf software that can be immediately used, instead, local privacy laws must be analyzed by PAs that intend to use VPP in order to elicit the privacy requirements to be enforced. Furthermore, such mechanism gives the VPP the possibility to be used outside the boundaries of GDPR.

The second critical point concerns the complexity of the organization to be protected. VPP, especially the Desktop Framework, has mechanisms to deal with such complexity, however, it is not only a matter of how large/wide an organization is, but also about the perspectives to be considered for the privacy analyses that will be performed by the VPP. Currently, the Desktop Framework considers social-organizational perspectives, business process perspectives, and security and privacy enforcement perspectives. Although we considered these perspectives to cover central assets of PA organizations, VPP may be extended to cover other perspectives such as threats or economic ones.

The empirical experiments, reported in this book, show that VPP is an effective platform. During its design, we faced many challenges: the results and the methods we used to face them are reported in this book.

Many people have contributed to the results of the project in many ways and their contribution has been essential in making VisiOn a successful project. We would like to thank for the hard work of all the participants of the project. In particular, we would like to thank the EU project officers who supported the project during its lifetime, and the reviewers who provided valuable feedback at the project reviews.

September 2020

Mattia Salnitri
Haralambos Mouratidis
Loredana Mancini
Paolo Giorgini

The original version of the book was revised: The name of the second editor has been corrected. The correction to the book is available at
https://doi.org/10.1007/978-3-030-59944-7_6

Acknowledgements

This research received funding from the European Union's Horizon 2020 research and innovation program under grant agreement No. 653642 - VisiOn.

Acronyms

EDPS	European Data Protection Supervisor
GDPR	General Data Protection Regulation
PA	Public Administration
EU	European Union
PNR	Passenger Name Record
EDPB	European Data Protection Board
DPO	Data Protection Officer
COD	Co-decision procedure
IRC	Internet Relay Chat
SMS	Short Message Service
CIA	Confidentiality, Integrity and Availability
DPIA	Data Protection Impact Assessment
CNIL	Commission Nationale de l'Informatique et des Libertés
ICT	Information and Communication Technologies
PLA	Privacy Level Agreement
VPP	VisiOn Privacy Platform
PbD	Privacy by Design
RE	Requirements Engineering
SoT	Separation of Tasks
BoT	Binding of Tasks
NtK	Necessity to know
AHP	Analytic Hierarchy Process
E-U	End-User
SID	System Integrator
R-C	Research and Academic
C	Citizen
DFD	Data Flow Diagram
PET	Privacy Enhancing Technology
EKD	Enterprise Knowledge Development
PMRM	Privacy Management Reference Model and Methodology
PRIPARE	PReparing Industry to Privacy-by-design by supporting its Application in REsearch
UML	Unified Modelling Language
GUI	Graphical User Interface
STS-ml	Socio Technical Security - modelling language
SecBPMN2	Secure Business Process Modelling Notation 2.0
SecBPMN2-ml	SecBPMN2- modelling language
SecBPMN2-Q	SecBPMN2- Query language

MoA	Municipality of Athens
IDS	Intrusion Detection System
RABAC	Role-Attribute-based Access Control
IDE	Integrated Development Environment
CSB	Communication Service Bus
DPI	Deep Packet Inspection
ATA	American Telemedicine Association's
EHR	Electronic Health Record
OPBG	spedale Pediatrico Bambino Gesu'
HIUNJ	Hospital Infantil Universitario Niño Jesus
MACS	Municipality of Athens Computer System
PAC	Privacy Assessment Component
PRC	Privacy Requirements Component
PSC	Privacy Specification Component
PRTC	Privacy Run-Time Component
PVC	Privacy Visualization Component
VDB	VisiOn DataBase
DAE	Dynamic Audit Engine
DVT	Data Value Tool
CVC	Citizen Visualisation Component
ViTo	Visualization Tool
IT	Information Technology
CARiSMA	CompliAnce, Risk, and Security Model Analyzer
MANE	TO BE DEFINED
PAE	Privacy Agreement Enforcer
STS-Tool	Socio Technical Security-Tool
CoA	City of Athens
GQM	Goal Question Metric
CIPAQ	"Credito d'Imposta Per l'Assunzione di personale Qualificato", transl.: "Tax credits for hiring skilled personnel"

Contents

An Introduction to Privacy

Andrea Praitano[1(✉)], Luca Giovannetti[2], Vasiliki Diamantopoulou[3], and Mattia Salnitri[4]

[1] Maticmind S.p.A., Via Mario Carucci 131, 00143 Rome, Italy
andrea.praitano@business-e.it
[2] ISC Information Sharing Company s.r.l, Via Paolo Emilio 7, 00192 Rome, Italy
l.giovannetti@gruppoisc.com
[3] University of the Aegean, Palama 2, 83200 Karlovassi, Samos, Greece
vdiamant@aegean.gr
[4] Politecnico di Milano, Via Ponzio, 34/5, 20133 Milan, Italy
mattia.salnitri@polimi.it

1 Introduction

During the last years data became a central asset for more and more of companies, where it is used to reach their business objectives. For example, stock exchange companies intensively use historical data on transactions to foresee the trend of the market; companies that have direct interactions with people customize their services based on the data about behaviour of customers.

One of the most precious type of data managed by companies, is personal information, i.e., information that can be linked to persons and can be used, for example, for profiling of targeted advertisement.

Luckily such wild usage of data has been limited by privacy laws. However, laws had substantial differences [12] allowing companies to exploit weak points based on how they want to process such data. Before May 2018, each state of European Union had its own privacy law and companies were allow to process data of all European Union (EU) citizens using the privacy law of the state where the headquarters where placed. This allowed companies to, essentially, chose the privacy law most suited to their data processing.

Luckily in May 2018 the European Union adopted a unified privacy law called General Data Protection Regulation (GDPR), which unifies the privacy laws of the EU member states and adopts novel concepts of protection in order to regulate the new massive usage of information and, specifically, of personal data. GDPR regulates the management of personal data and defines severe financial consequences if such regulation is broken. Nevertheless, many organizations and companies are not yet ready to handle personal data and demonstrate that the data are managed as specify by GDPR.

This section analyses GDPR, and in particular the privacy by design concept, i.e., how to create systems compliant with privacy regulation right from its design. After that, it describes an approach, used as basis for the rest of the book, where privacy agreements between users and organizations are specified as a form of contract.

© Springer Nature Switzerland AG 2020
M. Salnitri et al. (Eds.): Visual Privacy Management, LNCS 12030, pp. 1–21, 2020.
https://doi.org/10.1007/978-3-030-59944-7_1

2   Privacy Law Analysis

This section describes the contexts of the GDPR and the main concepts (called pillars) on which it is based.

2.1   Evolution of the European Data Protection Law

In 2016, after a long discussion for the finalization of the update process, the European Parliament and the Commission approved the first part of the new European Data Protection framework that will replace the "old" Directive 95/46/EC [6]. The update of the legislation had become no longer extendable because the world has changed dramatically since the approval of the Directive and there was the need to take a further step in a homogenization among the different European member states. Its approval was the first step taken by the European Union towards a standardization of data protection legislation that had arisen several years earlier in some of the member states but in a different form. One of the objectives of this directive, in addition of raising the level of protection of personal data of European citizens, consists in facilitating the free movement of data between the different Member States of the European Union. The two main objectives of Directive 95/46/EC consist in: (i) raising the level of protection of personal data of European citizens; (ii) facilitating the free movement of data between the different Member States of the Union. This is reported in the article 1 of the Directive related to "Object of the Directive" where in the first paragraph the protection of the personal data is described while the second paragraph specifies that the movement of personal data in the European Union could not be prohibited. This second point is important to well understand the Directive 95/46/EC, i.e. the previous privacy law, and the new European Data Protection framework. The right to data protection must balance with the necessity for the movement of the data.

The need to take a second step in the homogenization of the regulations between the different states of the European Union stems from the fact that the old European legislation was issued in the form of Directive, therefore each Member State has implemented it through national legislation.

2.2   European's Privacy Law Context

The European's privacy law context is composed by many different parts. The fundamental of the European privacy is in the Charter of Fundamental Rights of the European Union [22] and in the Articles 7 and 8 and in European Convention on Human Rights (Article 8).

The text of the Article 7 of the Charter is:

> *Article 7: Respect for private and family life*
> *Everyone has the right to respect for his or her private and family life, home and communications.*

The text of the Article 8 is:

Article 8: Protection of personal data

1. *Everyone has the right to the protection of personal data concerning him or her.*
2. *Such data must be processed fairly for specified purposes and on the basis of the consent of the person concerned or some other legitimate basis laid down by law. Everyone has the right of access to data which has been collected concerning him or her, and the right to have it rectified.*
3. *Compliance with these rules shall be subject to control by an independent authority.*

These rights are two of the fundamental for the European Union along with *Human dignity* (Article 1), *Right to life* (Article 2), *Right to the integrity of the person* (Article 3), *Prohibition of torture and inhuman or degrading treatment or punishment* (Article 4), *Prohibition of slavery and forced labour* (Article 5) and *Right to liberty and security* (Article 6). The right of privacy and data protection is one of the fundamentals for the European citizens. Around this fundamental right was approved the GDPR [17] that is the direct evolution of the Directive (EC) 46/95. The GDPR is a general regulation on data protection that can applied in all situations. The articles of Charter of Fundamental Rights of the European Union and the GDPR is the "core" of the European's data protection framework. These two elements apply to any situation and context. These apply to both public administrations and private organizations and are independent of the size and the sector in which they operate. The elements of the core of the framework give the general rules, then other regulations are added, for specific and sectorial type. The sense of the "general" in the name of this regulation is in this way, the general rules of data protection must be the same for the management of sensitive data in a hospital to a management of personal data in a non-profit association. The GDPR include indication on general principles for the protection of personal data in information systems and in traditional processes (Fig. 1).

The GDPR is integrated with different laws like Directive (EU) 2016/680 [4], Directive (EU) 2016/681 [5] and the Proposal for ePrivacy regulation [8]. The Directive (EU) 2016/680 is an integration of the GDPR in relation of the protection of natural persons regarding the processing of personal data by competent authorities for the purposes of the prevention, investigation, detection or prosecution of criminal offences or the execution of criminal penalties, including the safeguarding against and the prevention of threats to public security (Art. 1). The Directive (EU) 2016/681 is related to a specific type of personal data, the Passenger Name Record (PNR). At the same way the Proposal for Regulation on Privacy and Electronic Communications (ePrivacy regulation) is an integration of the GDPR in relation of the provision and use of electronic communications services (Art. 1). These European laws (in form of directive or regulation) represent the new European privacy Framework. This framework has a stable core

Fig. 1. Composition of the new European's data protection framework

(Article 8 and GDPR) that include the general principles and the direction for the data protection, the external parts could change faster to the other parts. For example, the Art. 28 of the Proposal for ePrivacy regulation specifies: "No later than three years after the date of application of this Regulation, and every three years thereafter, the Commission shall carry out an evaluation of this Regulation and present the main findings to the European Parliament, the Council and the European Economic and Social Committee. The evaluation shall, where appropriate, inform a proposal for the amendment or repeal of this Regulation in light of legal, technical or economic developments.". This is connected to the fact that the proposal is related to the electronic communications and they change vary fast.

> *The world in the end of '90, when the Directive 95/46 EC was approved, was very different of the modern world. Smartphones did not yet exist and the Internet connection was 56 Kbit/s. The firsts Internet searcher arrived on the market (Yahoo - 1994 and Google - 1997). The social networks had arrived only ten years after (Facebook - 2004). About the messaging, Internet Relay Chat (IRC) was created 1988 and the mobile messaging was based on Short Message Service (SMS).*

Another important part of the European Data Protection framework is composed by the opinions from the European Data Protection Board (EDPB) (ex "Article 29 Working Party")[1], established by Article 68 of the GDPR. It provides the European Commission with independent advice on data protection matters and helps in the development of harmonised policies for data protection in the EU Member States. This board is composed of representatives of the:

- national supervisory authorities in the Member States;
- European Data Protection Supervisor (EDPS);
- European Commission.

The role of the European Data Protection Board is in line with the main goal of the GDPR. The main responsibilities of the Board are related to the homogenisation in the application of the data protection through the European members.

2.3   The Main Pillars of the GDPR

The GDPR is based on nine main concepts (called pillar), as shown in Fig. 2. In the following we briefly describe them.

Fig. 2. The European data protection pillars

The **first pillar** is the territorial scope of the GDPR (Art. 3 of GDPR). The change in the scope from the previous included in the Directive 46/95 EC to the new one is related to align the law to the globalisation and interconnection between the economies. This point has been dealt in many publications and articles therefore it is not addressed again here.

The **second pillar** is the accountability of the data controller (Art. 5 of GDPR). This is an important change because the risk-based approach is in line

---

[1] https://edpb.europa.eu.

with the common security/cyber security best practices. The Data Protection by Design, by Default and Data Protection Impact Assessment's pillars could be consider as direct consequences of the data controller's accountability.

The **third pillar** are the data subjects' rights (from Art. 12 to 21 of GDPR). The new European Data Protection framework include many different rights. The basic concept is that the owner of personal data is the data subject, the data controller uses these data but the ownership of these data remains in the data subject. The data subject has the right to maintain the control on his/her data.

The **fourth pillar** is the Data Protection by Design principle (Art. 25 of GDPR). The application of this principle is that the protection of personal data is not an optional but it must be the standard approach for an organization. When an organization sees the need for a new treatment, it must be lawful and secure. The point of view for the security is not the organisation but is the data subject. This principle must implement also in the existing treatments.

The **fifth pillar** is the Data Protection by Default principle (Art. 25 of GDPR). The data subject is the owner of the personal data but he/she is the weaker part of the organization. The organisation must take in consideration the data subject's point of view.

The **sixth pillar** is the Data Protection Impact Assessment (Art. 35 of GDPR). This principle is son of the accountability of the data controller, it manages the personal data and receives benefits from this activity; as it receives benefits it has the responsibility of going to protect them by deciding the security measures it deems appropriate to implement.

The **seventh pillar** is the role of Data Protection Officer (DPO) in the organisation (from Art. 37 to 39 of GDPR). In some cases, the data controller must appoint a Data Protection Officer to control the state of data protection in the organisation. The DPO is a sort of internal data protection consultant and auditor that help the organisation to take the right way for the data protection. Usually the data controller experience is not connected to the data protection but is related to the business of the organisation, the DPO helps the data controller to know the right situation on the data protection in the data controller's organisation.

The **eighth pillar** is the formalisation of the European Data Protection Board (Art. 68 of GDPR) already described in the previous section.

The **ninth pillar** is the Data breach (Art. 33 and 34 of GDPR). The Art. 33 defined that the data controller must to notify to supervisory authority when it suffers a data breach. In fact, the data controller must self-disclose within 72 h to the supervisory authority. Data breaches should not be hidden under the carpet but addressed and managed. The Art. 34 defined that in some specific cases the data controller must self-disclose within 72 h to the data subjects.

With more and more personal and confidential information stored, shared and managed at digital level, it is expected from both the individuals and the organisations that appropriate measures should be implemented to ensure privacy. The satisfactions of the rights of data subjects imposed by the GDPR is not a straightforward process. It requires a lot of effort both by the organisations and the individuals.

2.4   Privacy and Electronic Communications (ePrivacy) Regulation

Some of the pillars of the GDPR are based on the ePrivacy regulation [8]. Such Regulation is the update of the Directive 2002/58/EC [3], called "ePrivacy Directive". This new regulation is based on a consultation and impact assessment organised by the European Commission. The key findings are the following (from the 2017/0003 Co-decision procedure (COD) [7]):

1. Need for special rules for the electronic communications sector on confidentiality of electronic communications
2. Extension of scope to new communications services (Over the Top - OTTs)
3. Amending the exemptions to consent for processing traffic and location data
4. Support for solutions proposed to the cookie consent issue

The feedback from citizens and civil society organisations can be synthesized in a request of more protection on digital personal data and metadata and more security on *the top services*, i.e. services provided over other services of the same or from a different service provider. This regulation adds to the GDPR some specific rules on the treatment and protection of digital personal data stored in the citizens' terminals and in the service providers' systems but also the data subjects' metadata. One of the important aspects introduced by the ePrivacy regulation is that each data subject can provide and revoke the consent to the controller in an easy way, and they have the right to revoke the consent in the same way they provided it.

3   Data Protection by Design

When designing a system that requires meeting a security quality attribute, system architects need to consider the scope of security needs and the minimum required security qualities. Not every system will need all of the basic security and privacy principles but will use one or more in combination based on the domain, the type of information that will be manged and the performance required by the system-to-be. The definition of a minimum level of security and privacy must be defined when a system is designed since such requirements must be factored with the other quality attributes.

3.1   The Story of Data Protection by Design Principle

The principle of Data Protection by Design is new in European Union, the GDPR introduced in 2016, with its approval, this principle in the new European Data Protection framework. The first statement of this principle dates back to 1995 [13], by Ms. Ann Cavoukian member of the Information and Privacy Commissioner of Ontario, Canada. The first statement of this principle followed of only one year the old Directive 95/46 EC. In 2010 the 32nd international conference of Data Protection and Privacy Commissioners/Authorities held in Jerusalem formalized these points:

1. Recognize Privacy by Design as an essential component of fundamental privacy protection;
2. Encourage the adoption of Privacy by Design's Foundational Principles, such as those set out below as guidance to establishing privacy as an organization's default mode of operation;
3. Invite Data Protection and Privacy Commissioners/Authorities to:
   a. promote Privacy by Design, as widely as possible through distribution of materials, education and personal advocacy;
   b. foster the incorporation of the Privacy by Design Foundational Principles in the formulation of privacy policy and legislation within their respective jurisdictions;
   c. proactively encourage research on Privacy by Design;
   d. consider adding Privacy by Design to the agendas of events taking place on International Data Privacy Day (January 28);
   e. report back to the 33rd International Data Protection and Privacy Commissioners Conference, where appropriate, on Privacy by Design activities and initiatives undertaken within their jurisdictions with a view to sharing best practices.

Such principles were new for Europe but they were already considered 20 years before in other parts of the world. For example, the Canadian's enunciation of Privacy by Design principle include seven "foundational principles":

1. proactive not reactive; preventative not remedial;
2. privacy as the default setting;
3. privacy embedded into design;
4. full functionality - positive-sum, not zero-sum;
5. end-to-end security - full lifecycle protection;
6. visibility and transparency - keep it open;
7. respect for user privacy - keep it user-centric.

In the following sections we will analyze the European Data Protection framework to understand how to implement the principles defined in the GDPR.

3.2 A Possible Approach to Data Protection by Design Based on Best Practices and Standards

The Data Protection by Design has three main references in the European law, the first is in the Article 25 of the GDPR, the second is in the Article 20 of the Directive 680/2016 and the last one is in the draft of the ePrivacy Regulation (recital 23). To understand well we need to analyse these points of the laws. We can start from the draft of ePrivacy Regulation.

> *(23) The principles of data protection by design and by default were codified under Article 25 of Regulation (EU) 2016/679.*

The draft of ePrivacy Regulation refers to the GDPR regarding the Data Protection by Design. The article 25 of GDPR and the Article 20 of Directive 680/2016 have a similar formulation. We analyse in detail the Article 25 of GDPR.

> *Taking into account the state of the art, the cost of implementation and the nature, scope, context and purposes of processing as well as the risks of varying likelihood and severity for rights and freedoms of natural persons posed by the processing, the controller shall, both at the time of the determination of the means for processing and at the time of the processing itself, implement appropriate technical and organisational measures, such as pseudonymisation, which are designed to implement data-protection principles, such as data minimisation, in an effective manner and to integrate the necessary safeguards into the processing in order to meet the requirements of this Regulation and protect the rights of data subjects.*

To understand the Data protection by Design principle we need to analyse and consider:

- the state of the art;
- the cost of implementation;
- how to implement appropriate technical measures;
- how to implement appropriate organisational measures;
- data-protection principles.

The first two bullets points, i.e., "State of the art" and "Cost of implementation" define frequently two opposite direction of design. The most modern security measures are expensive and may not be suitable for the organization.

The "data-protection principles" to be considered when reading Article 25, is linked to the Article 5 of GDPR which specifies:

> *[..] (f) processed in a manner that ensures appropriate security of the personal data, including protection against unauthorised or unlawful processing and against accidental loss, destruction or damage, using appropriate technical or organisational measures ("integrity and confidentiality").*

The personal data processing has to ensures the appropriate level of security. The Article 32 in the Sect. 2 (Security of personal data) of GDPR explain some aspects of security of personal data processing.

> *Taking into account the state of the art, the costs of implementation and the nature, scope, context and purposes of processing as well as the risk of varying likelihood and severity for the rights and freedoms of natural persons, the controller and the processor shall implement appropriate technical and organisational measures to ensure a level of security appropriate to the risk, including inter alia as appropriate:*
>
> 1. *the pseudonymisation and encryption of personal data;*
> 2. *the ability to ensure the ongoing confidentiality, integrity, availability and resilience of processing systems and services;*
> 3. *the ability to restore the availability and access to personal data in a timely manner in the event of a physical or technical incident;*
> 4. *a process for regularly testing, assessing and evaluating the effectiveness of technical and organisational measures for ensuring the security of the processing.*
>
> *In assessing the appropriate level of security account shall be taken in particular of the risks that are presented by processing, in particular from accidental or unlawful destruction, loss, alteration, unauthorised disclosure of, or access to personal data transmitted, stored or otherwise processed.*

In particular, the article specifies that an organization has to guarantee the Confidentiality, Integrity, Availability and Resilience of processing system and services that use personal data. The organization, moreover, has to set up a "security testing process" that evaluate regularly the efficient and effectiveness of the security measures. The security of personal data is not "static" but dynamic because the security measures defined today are not efficient and effectiveness tomorrow and the organization has to have the capacity to align the security measures to the state of art.

3.3 Application of the Privacy by Design Principles

The principle of Privacy by Design introduced by the European regulation concerning the protection of personal data, companies and public administration requires a proactive approach to data protection and no longer responsive, making it necessary to provide for operating modes, configuration and security measures can safeguard the Confidentiality, Integrity and Availability (CIA) of personal data "by default" or when they "enter" in the organization. To conform to the principle of Privacy by Design is necessary to integrate them, at least, with the following activities:

- identification of the flow of personal information and treatments that will be subjected throughout their life cycle within the organization
- identification punctually the security requirements that the applications and the technological infrastructure to support must meet in order to protect personal data, CIA in any State they are located

- programming standards that allow to implement applications free from vulnerabilities caused by unsafe
- programming standards architecture needed to meet the security requirements defined definition of masking techniques (or similar) of personal data if you provide for use in environments other than production (testing, training, ...)
- integration of test plans with tasks of verifying the correct implementation of security requirements defined at both application infrastructure
- predict your testing efforts aimed at verifying the effectiveness of the security measures and application and architectural standards implemented (ethical hacking, penetration testing, vulnerability assessment, code review, etc.)

3.4   A Practical Approach to Data Protection by Design Based on VisiOn Project Experience

Before addressing the application of the principle, we must understand the reasons why we must protect information within the organization. There are different motivations, both external and internal to the organization, that deems the protection of information, based on the type of information that have to be protected. Personal information must be protected as specified in the personal data protection of GDPR: information relating to an identified or identifiable natural person must be protected. But there are other type of data, not related to natural person, that must be protected, for example information about a company or industrial secrets or patent information (Table 1).

In a real organization there are technical and organization security measures that aims to protect relevant information. This level of basic security is distributed to the entire organization without taking into consideration the type of data processed. Some example of these security measures includes:

- Definition of a Data Protection Policy for the Organization;
- Definition and assignment of roles;
- Data Protection Management System;
- Process of authorization of logical and physical accesses;
- Physical security of the organization's building(s);
- Basic Logical Access system;
- Antivirus, Antimalware and Antispam systems;
- Network segregation;
- Monitoring;
- Patch management process;
- Event and Incident Management Process;

Organizations can implement a second, more specific, level of security measures that target only personal data processing and systems. This level includes:

- Formalization of processors;
- Authorized persons;

Table 1. Example of security measures to protect CIA parameters

Parameter	Possible security measures
Confidentiality is the degree to which access to information is restricted to a defined group authorized to have this access	• Access to information is granted on a need to know basis • Employees take measures to ensure that information does not find its way to those people who do not need it • Logical access management ensures that unauthorized persons or processes do not have access to automated systems, databases and programs. A user, for example, can not change the settings of the PC • A segregation of duties is created between the system development organization, the processing organization and the user's organization. A system developer cannot, for example, make any changes to salaries • Strict segregation rules are created between the development environment, the test and acceptance environment and the production environment • In the processing and use of data, measures are taken to ensure the privacy of personnel and third parties • The use of computers by end users is surrounded by measures so that the confidentiality of the information is guaranteed
Integrity is the degree to which the information is up to date and without errors, this includes the Correctness and the Completeness of information	• Changes in systems and data are authorized • Where possible, mechanisms are built in that force people to use the correct term • Users' actions are recorded (logged) so that it can be determined who made a change in the information • Vital system actions, for example, installing new software, cannot be carried out by just one person. By segregating duties, positions and authorities, at least two people will be necessary to carry out a change that has major consequences • The integrity of data can be ensured to a large degree through encryption techniques, which protects the information from unauthorized access or change. The policy and management principles for encryption can be defined in a separate policy document
Availability is the degree to which information can be retrieved by the user from the system	• The management and storage of data is such that the chance of losing information is minimal • Backup procedures are set up. The regulatory requirements for how long data must be stored are taken into account. The location of the backup is separated physically from the business in order to ensure the availability in cases of emergency • Emergency procedures are set up to ensure that the activities can resume as soon as possible after a large-scale disruption

- Access logging collector system;
- Data breach identification, escalation, evaluation and notification process;
- Data Subject's rights Management Process;

Each data processing (bot for personal and for not personal data) can integrate extra security measures, if necessary. The Fig. 3 explain graphically the different steps of security measures.

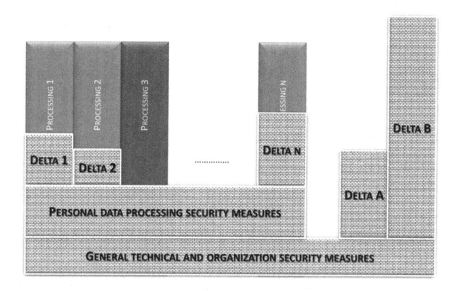

Fig. 3. Security measures in the organization

For the identification of extra security measures for personal data processing the GDPR give some requirements. It is possible design a sort of process for the definition of extra security measures for personal data processing. The steps are:

Step 1: Identification of a new personal data processing. The organization identified an opportunity to do some of new for the organization, before the implementing of the activity the organization must evaluate the potential impact of rights and freedoms of data subjects.

Step 2: Identification of the personal data processed in the new processing. The organization execute a data mapping to understand the type of personal data processed in the new processing and where this data will be used.

Step 3: Evaluation of the processing risk (based on WP29 op. 248). The organization must evaluate if the processing has a high risk for data subjects.

Step 4: Execution of the Data Protection Impact Assessment on the high-risk processing. Before the implementation the high-risk processing has evaluate through a Data Protection Impact Assessment (DPIA) to evaluate if the risk for the data subjects is too high for the processing implementation.

Step 5: Risk analysis execution on the processing and its supporting systems. The DPIA is performed to evaluate the level of residual risk on the data subjects. The DPIA does not take in consideration the organization point of view (e.g. economic losses, loss of corporate image, etc.). The risk analysis is performed by the organization point of view and produce a list of security and data protection requirements for the processing and its supporting systems.

Step 6: Development of the processing and systems. The development of the processing and its supporting system based on functional requirements' list and security and data protection requirements list.

Step 7: Execution of security tests. Before the official go live of processing and systems the organization must test the quality of functionality (based on functional requirements) and security (based on security and data protection requirements).

Step 8: Go live of the new processing. The go live of the new processing include the registration of the new processing and related information in the Record of processing activities.

4   The State of the Art in the Data Protection European Market

The description of the state of art of the frameworks and technologies aligned to the new European Data Protection framework is not easy. There are many kinds of frameworks that can support the new European Data Protection framework. We can divide the frameworks in different macro types:

1. Frameworks for support the execution of some GDPR's activities (e.g. the execution of DPIA, Data Protection by Design, etc.);
2. Frameworks that can support the Data Protection process and governance;
3. Frameworks for support the data subjects' rights (e.g. the request of Right of access);
4. Frameworks that guarantee the Personal Data portability;
5. Frameworks for data breach identification;
6. Encryption and anonymization/pseudo anonymization frameworks;
7. Security frameworks for the data protection.

From the above list there are some types of frameworks that are on the market from many years (e.g. security frameworks, encryption tools, data breach identification, etc.), some other frameworks are new or are an evolution of existing tools (e.g. manage of data subjects' requests could be a penalization of a trouble ticketing tool and the organization could be identify the data subjects' request as a specific type of service request). The last category of frameworks includes all typical security tools (e.g. Antivirus, firewall, IPS, IDS, SIEM, etc.). These frameworks are not specific for the new European data protection framework.

The first two classes of tools, at the moment of writing this chapter, are very dynamic. There are a lot of software tools in the market and there are many new software houses that are developing tools for the GDPR compliance. For example, there is project related to DPIA supported by Commission Nationale de l'Informatique et des Libertés (CNIL) [2]; this is the tool based on the CNIL methodology for the execution of DPIA [18–20]. This is an example for the practical execution of the DPIA based on a National Data Protection Authority guideline. The GDPR does not require the use of tools to ensure compliance, but it is undeniable that the use of tools can help to ensure and maintain compliance with the legislation in a simpler way.

5   Privacy Level Agreement

The advances and the rapid development in the domain of Information and Communication Technologies (ICT) have led to their adoption by organizations, enabling them to transform their services to electronic services (e-services), increasing thus their efficiency, productivity and growth [11]. Emphasis is given on security and privacy of the Information Technology (IT) systems when they are used for the management of personal data. During the development and operation of IT systems, security and privacy properties should be satisfied. This is even more imperative when IT systems are used by service providers who work and manage critical types of personal data (i.e. sensitive data), for example, health-related ones.

The necessity for the privacy-enabled management of personal data is also reflected in the GDPR, which aims to protect individuals' (or Data Subjects, according to the GDPR terminology) interests, imposing service providers' (or Data Controllers according to the GDPR terminology) to ensure data subjects' privacy and providing them the ownership and control of their data. In this context, it is crucial that Data Controllers' Information Systems are developed and operate in a way that improve transparency of Data Subjects' data sharing. Thus, it is important that Data Controllers are able to clearly specify Data Subjects' privacy needs, provide them with feedback on how their data is managed, stored, shared, etc. and on whether sharing of their data conflicts with their requirements. In addition, Data Controllers should enable Data Subjects to understand potential threats and vulnerabilities to their privacy requirements, as well as trust relationships that might endanger their privacy.

We address this challenge by proposing the use of the concept of Privacy Level Agreement (PLA) [9,10], which formalizes a mutual agreement of the privacy settings between an individual and an organization, where the former will commit to provide and maintain these settings throughout the provision of the service. Consequently, the use of PLAs allows Data Controllers to (i) handle the personal data they keep taking into account Data Subjects' privacy needs, (ii) provide information concerning the processes they follow regarding the management of personal data, and (iii) demonstrate that they have proceeded to all the necessary actions to make their systems robust, mitigating all possible threats. The adoption of this approach can enhance user's trust and confidence when using e-services, can improve transparency, by imposing accountability to Data Controllers, regarding protection of Data Subjects' information, and consequently, it contributes to confidence between Data Controllers and Data Subjects, since it provides a new type of Privacy Management System that allows the latter to take control over the data they provide, in order to take advantage of the e-services.

The PLA is delivered in a form of a structured agreement that consists of fields, each of them capturing important and obligatory information with regards to privacy of Data Subjects' personal data. It consists of two sections, the Data Controllers section and the Data Subjects section, which are described in the following subsections.

5.1   Data Controllers PLA Section

The Data Controllers section has the following fields. For each field we provide a short description.

Identity: This field describes the publication of Data Controller's name, place of establishment, and the contact details of the Data Controller's data administrator. Assigning such a responsibility to an employee of an organization, is important so that the individual has a point of contact in case they want to make a query, contributing to the accountability of the service [15].

Data: Specifies which personal data the Data Subject needs to provide to the Data Controller.

Data processing rights: Provides information about processing and storing of Data Subjects' data. Acquiring complete information about processing and storing of their personal data to the Data Controllers' Information Systems, Data Subjects are fully informed, e.g., on the location of their stored data, on the access and processing rights, etc.

Data Sharing Preferences: Provides information about third parties that can have access to Data Subjects' data, since as the Data Controller has the ability to collect huge amount of personal data, this may attract external parties that want to acquire these data [15] for purposes different from the ones that the data has been collected (e.g., for marketing actions).

Data Privacy Measures: Specifies the technical, physical and organizational measures in place to protect Data Subjects' personal data against accidental or unlawful destruction or loss, alteration, unauthorized use, modification, disclosure of access, and against all other unlawful forms of processing. These measures can ensure the satisfaction of the relevant privacy requirements that have been imposed.

Privacy Threat Analysis: Provides the threat analysis of the Data Controller's privacy needs and requirements. Data Subjects need assurances that the Data Controller introduces appropriate mechanisms and processes to support the privacy needs, and inform them when these needs are not followed due to either Data Controllers policies or the corresponding national or European legislation. Having such information improves the transparency of Data Controller's operations in terms of data management, and it therefore contributes to improve Data Subjects' trust.

Privacy Trust Analysis: Provides the trust analysis of the Data Controller's privacy needs and requirements. Since trust is considered a very important factor for the adoption of electronic services [21], Data Controllers have to demonstrate that the infrastructure and the staff responsible for the operation of this infrastructure can be trusted [14,16].

Law Compliance: Provides information on whether privacy requirements are complaint with privacy laws at a national and European level. In particular, it specifies the constraints imposed by regulations and laws and also how the Data Controller uses/manages Data Subjects' data. Also, it verifies if the data management specified by the Data Controller respects the constraints specified in laws and regulations.

5.2   Data Subjects PLA Section

The Data Subjects' section consists of the following fields: *National Public Authority*: Contains the details of the National Public Authority responsible for protecting Data Subjects' personal data rights. Adding such information to the PLA will raise the awareness of the Data Subjects about the protection of their data rights by the specific national public authority.

Data Subjects' Privacy Preferences: Contains the privacy preferences of the Data Subject that have been collected by the Data Controller. The study of [23] reveals that the government applications that engage individuals and allow interactivity with them, have positive payoffs for trust in government.

History Based Assessment: Consists of an analysis of the Data Subjects' privacy preferences and the generation of a prediction of the possible outcomes of subsequent requests. It contains an estimation of the accepted or denied requests for individuals data, based on their requirements available and the aggregated statistics about other Data Subjects, collected up to that moment.

Data Value: Contains the Data Subjects' perspective concerning their data and the valuation of Data Subjects' data by the Data Controller and the average valuation of all the Data Subjects. This information can increase transparency since it communicates to the Data Subject the relative value of data and consequently, it will increase the trust of then in the Data Controller.

5.3 Generation of the PLA

The adoption of the GDPR is a major concern for data controllers of the public and private sector, as they are obliged to conform to the new principles and requirements managing personal data. The concept of the PLA captures the privacy-related entities mentioned in the GDPR and the relationships among them, and allows the designers of e-services to better understand the concepts that must be included in a PLA.

The PLA is generated after a series of actions that have to be triggered by the Data Controller. More specifically, through the use of a platform able to support the analysis of privacy issues from different perspectives (i.e., organizational, business-process, threat, and trust), PLA can be realized. The VisiOn Privacy Platform (VPP) which has been designed and developed under a H2020 European Project[2], and will be thoroughly presented in the next chapters of the book, provides a holistic approach [1], covering all the potential aspects that influence and, consequently, shape the relationship in terms of trust between Data Subjects and online services provided by a Data Controller. VPP distinguishes two roles: Data Controller and Data Subjects. The Data Subject uses VPP's functionalities during run-time only, i.e. while using a service carried out by the Data Controller. The Data Controller uses VPP's functionalities during both, design-time and run-time of a system.

The Data Controller uses the platform to capture privacy requirements and composes questionnaires for Data Subjects, in order the PLA of each Data Subject to be created. On the other side, Data Subjects use the platform to specify their privacy preferences. The PLA, an example of it is depicted in Fig. 4, embodies the privacy policy that must be applied for each Data Subject.

VPP provides Data Controllers with the ability to create Data Subjects' PLAs using Data Subjects' privacy preferences, which are elicited through clear and non-technical questionnaires. Also, VPP enables Data Subjects to understand and realize the value of their data, using enhanced visualization elements, and use that value to determine their privacy preferences. Moreover, VPP brings together a set of software engineering methodologies and tools across different levels, from privacy requirements to run-time, and different perspectives, from data evaluation to privacy assurance. Such integration provides a clear advantage over existing software engineering approaches and tools, since it enables a holistic analysis of privacy needs that includes both Data Controllers and Data Subjects.

---

[2] http://www.visioneuproject.eu.

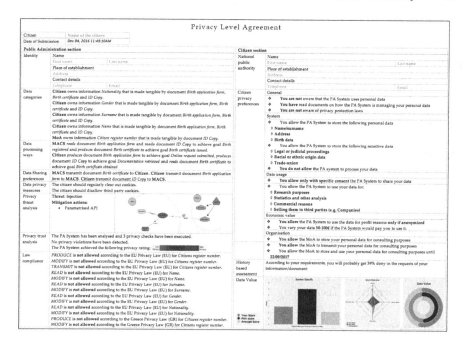

Fig. 4. PLA example

6 Conclusions

This chapter gives an overview of the complex problem of privacy. In particular it describes the law context and the complexity of creating a privacy aware system (privacy by design) and how to specify how personal data is managed in a system PLA.

These issues grow in complexity with the size of the system to be design or modified. In particular large systems such as the one used by Public Administration (PA) are extremely complex system that, nevertheless, must to adhere to the new privacy laws.

Such problems were the focus of the VisiOn European project whose objective was to create a platform to handle privacy in large system and give the possibility to the users of such systems to easily express their privacy preferences, in order to merge privacy requirements coming from experts with privacy requirements coming from the owners of the data manipulated. The objective of the project was not limited to the gathering of requirements but to their enforcement in the system analyzed.

The next chapters describe how the VisiOn Project created the platform, called VPP, and how the platform was evaluated.

Acronyms

EDPS European Data Protection Supervisor
GDPR General Data Protection Regulation
PA Public Administration
EU European Union
PNR Passenger Name Record
EDPB European Data Protection Board
DPO Data Protection Officer
COD Co-decision procedure
IRC Internet Relay Chat
SMS Short Message Service
CIA Confidentiality, Integrity and Availability
DPIA Data Protection Impact Assessment
CNIL Commission Nationale de l'Informatique et des Libertés
ICT Information and Communication Technologies
PLA Privacy Level Agreement
VPP VisiOn Privacy Platform
IT Information Technology

References

1. Angelopoulos, K., et al.: A holistic approach for privacy protection in e-government. In: Proceedings of the 12th International Conference on Availability, Reliability and Security, p. 17. ACM (2017)
2. CNIL. The open source PIA software helps to carry out data protection impact assesment (2018). https://www.cnil.fr/en/open-source-pia-software-helps-carry-out-data-protection-impact-assesment
3. European commission. Directive 2002/58/EC (2016). https://eur-lex.europa.eu/legal-content/EN/ALL/?uri=celex:32002L0058
4. European commission. Directive 2016/680 (2016). https://eur-lex.europa.eu/legal-content/EN/TXT/?uri=celex:32016L0680
5. European commission. Directive 2016/680 (2016). https://eur-lex.europa.eu/eli/dir/2016/681/oj?uri=CELEX:32016L0681
6. European commission. Directive 95/46/EC (1995). https://eur-lex.europa.eu/legal-content/EN/TXT/?uri=celex:31995L0046
7. European commission. Procedure 2017/0003/COD (2017). https://eur-lex.europa.eu/procedure/EN/2017_3
8. European commission. Proposal for a REGULATION OF THE EUROPEAN PARLIAMENT AND OF THE COUNCIL concerning the respect for private life and the protection of personal data in electronic communications and repealing Directive 2002/58/EC (Regulation on Privacy and Electronic Communications) (2016). https://eur-lex.europa.eu/legal-content/EN/TXT/?uri=CELEX:52017PC0010
9. Diamantopoulou, V., Pavlidis, M., Mouratidis, H.: Privacy level agreements for public administration information systems (2017)
10. Diamantopoulou, V., et al.: Privacy data management and awareness for public administrations: a case study from the healthcare domain. In: Schweighofer, E., Leitold, H., Mitrakas, A., Rannenberg, K. (eds.) Annual Privacy Forum. LNCS, vol. 10518, pp. 192–209. Springer, Cham (2017). https://doi.org/10.1007/978-3-319-67280-9_11

11. Zakareya Ebrahim and Zahir Irani: E-government adoption: architecture and barriers. Bus. Process Manage. J. **11**(5), 589–611 (2005)
12. Grynwajc, S.: Privacy at the crossroads: a comparative analysis of regulation in the US, the EU and Canada (2015)
13. Hes, R., Borking, J.: Privacy enhancing technologies: the path to anonymity, p. 12 (1998). ISBN 90.74087
14. Horst, M., Kuttschreuter, M., Gutteling, J.M.: Perceived usefulness, personal experiences, risk perception and trust as determinants of adoption of e-government services in The Netherlands. Comput. Hum. Behav. **23**(4), 1838–1852 (2007)
15. Marche, S., McNiven, J.D.: E-government and e-governance: the future isn't what it used to be. Can. J. Adm. Sci./Revue Canadienne des Sciences de l'Administration **20**(1), 74–86 (2003)
16. Milloy, M., Fink, D., Morris, R.: Modeling online security and privacy to increase consumer purchasing intent. In: Informing Science & IT Education Joint Conference (InSITE) (2002)
17. The European Parliament and the Council of the European Union. REGULATION (EU) 2016/679 OF THE EUROPEAN PARLIAMENT AND OF THE COUNCIL (2016). http://ec.europa.eu/justice/data-protection/reform/files/regulation_oj_en.pdf
18. Privacy Impact Assessment (PIA) – Knowledge Bases. Technical report CNIL (2018)
19. Privacy Impact Assessment (PIA) – Methodology. Technical report CNIL (2018)
20. Privacy Impact Assessment (PIA) – Templates. Technical report. CNIL (2018)
21. Srivastava, S.C., Teo, T.: Citizen trust development for e-government adoption: case of Singapore. In: PACIS 2005 Proceedings, p. 59 (2005)
22. European Union. Consolidated Versions of the Treaty on European Union and of the Treaty on the Functioning of the European Union: Charter of Fundamental Rights of the European Union. Office for Official publications of the European Communities (2010)
23. Welch, E.W., Hinnant, C.C., Moon, M.J.: Linking citizen satisfaction with e-government and trust in government. J. Public Adm. Res. Theor. **15**(3), 371–391 (2004)

A Holistic Approach for Privacy Requirements Analysis: An Industrial Case Study

Mohamad Gharib[1]([⊠]), Paolo Giorgini[2], Mattia Salnitri[3], Elda Paja[2], Haralambos Mouratidis[4], Michalis Pavlidis[4], and Jose Fran. Ruiz[5]

[1] University of Florence, Firenze, Italy
mohamad.gharib@unifi.it
[2] University of Trento, Trento, Italy
{paolo.giorgini,elda.paja}@unitn.it
[3] Politecnico di Milano, Milan, Italy
mattia.salnitri@polimi.it
[4] University of Brighton, Brighton, UK
{H.Mouratidis,M.Pavlidis}@brighton.ac.uk
[5] ATOS, Madrid, Spain
jose.ruizr@atos.net

1 Introduction

Privacy is becoming more and more a prominent concern for most countries, particularly for those of them that are moving toward the implementation of e-government [18] where software systems dealing with personal information (i.e., citizens, customers, etc.) have to be compliant with national and international privacy laws [26]. Moreover, while privacy has been frequently identified as a main concern for Public Administrations (PAs) while dealing with citizens' information for performing their activities and providing services [18,43], several recent studies have shown that citizens might refrain from using services when their privacy is endangered [49,56]. According to Spiekermann et al. [72], *an increasing majority of US and EU citizens say that existing laws and organizational practices do not provide a reasonable level of privacy protection and that companies share personal information inappropriately.* As an answer, the new European Privacy directives [14] introduced a number of privacy-related rules to increase the citizens' trust in PAs and their services. Despite this, organizations still suffer from several shortcomings that can endanger citizens' information such as bad security practices, hacker and, most importantly, insider attacks, data thefts, etc. [1].

As advocated by Privacy by Design (PbD) [12,37], to ensure a certain level of privacy we need to adopt a systematic and holistic approach to privacy requirements engineering. More specifically, privacy requirements should be considered as first class requirements along with functional and non-functional ones [17]. For decades, privacy requirements have been considered the result of a security analysis (e.g., [37,52,82]) and specified as generic non-functional requirements without any clear measure for their satisfaction [3,52,81]. Only recently,

© Springer Nature Switzerland AG 2020
M. Salnitri et al. (Eds.): Visual Privacy Management, LNCS 12030, pp. 22–53, 2020.
https://doi.org/10.1007/978-3-030-59944-7_2

the research community proposed a number of approaches to privacy requirements engineering [12,37], but without showing their effectiveness in real cases and without considering privacy requirements for already existing systems (e.g., [21,78]), as we usually have in PAs.

On the other hand, privacy is an elusive and vague concept [22,68], and it is hard to reach consensus on its definition [22]. Although several efforts have been made to clarify this concept by linking it to more concrete concepts such as secrecy, personhood, control of personal information, etc. [69], there is no consensus on the definition of these concepts or which of them should be used to analyze privacy [24,69]. This adds more complexity while eliciting, classifying, prioritizing, and validating privacy requirements. In addition, the relations between privacy requirements and other types of requirements have not been extensively studied, i.e., it is not clear how privacy requirements can be linked to other types of requirements.

In this chapter, we propose a holistic approach for analyzing privacy requirements specialized in their eliciting, classifying, prioritizing, and validating. The approach follows the experience we gained in the Vision Project, an H2020 innovation action funded by the European Commission (Visual Privacy Management in User Centric Open Requirements) [26]. Specifically, in the project we built on the idea that PAs can be engaged as the main source for defining the privacy requirements of users responsible for managing citizens' information, while citizens can considered as the main source for defining the privacy requirements of information owners. In other words, our approach gives citizens (information owners) a voice while specifying their privacy preferences, along those of the PAs as required by privacy norms. With our proposal, we aim at assisting software engineers in designing privacy-aware systems by providing the guidance and support while eliciting, classifying, prioritizing, and validating/consolidating privacy requirements.

The rest of the chapter is organized as follows. Section 2 presents the research baseline. In Sect. 3, we present our approach for privacy requirements specification, while Sect. 4 discusses how the approach has been used to specify the VisiOn privacy requirements. In Sect. 5, we discuss threats to approach validity. We present related work in Sect. 6 and, finally, we conclude the chapter and discuss future work in Sect. 7.

2   Research Baseline

A main goal of requirements engineering is discovering stakeholders' actual needs that drive to requirements for the system-to-be [8]. This requires a well-defined systematic process to be followed while dealing with such needs. Several Requirements Engineering (RE) processes for dealing with stakeholders' needs have been proposed (e.g., [40,57,70,71,74]) and most of them include the following activities: elicitation, classification, prioritization, and validation. In the rest of this section, we list and discuss the main contributions in each of these activities.

Requirements elicitation is one of the first activities in RE process and can be defined as the process of discovering, acquiring, and elaborating requirements for the system-to-be through consulting relevant stakeholders, investigating the system's documentation and/or using domain knowledge [40,70,71]. Usually, requirements elicitation is a complex and iterative process that starts with requirements discovery and ends with requirements documentation [70,83]. Requirements elicitation is one of the most critical activities in the RE process (e.g., [8,70,83]), since getting the right requirements is considered a key factor for software development projects [36]. The main idea of requirements elicitation is gathering stakeholders' requirements concerning the system-to-be. Therefore, involving stakeholders in the process is essential for the process to succeed [8]. However, involving them is not an easy task, since stakeholders, usually, express their requirements in very general terms, they may have conflicting requirements, and they may change their requirements during the analysis process [42,70]. Thus, involving stakeholders does not always guarantee the elicitation of the right requirements. Several requirements elicitation approaches and techniques have been proposed in the literature, including interviews [2], questionnaires [20], task analysis [11], introspection [29], laddering [34], requirements workshop [83], ethnography [6], apprenticing [9], scenarios [83], and prototyping [70]. A new trend is the use of serious games (gamifications) in which game-based elements are used during the requirements elicitation process [7,19,61]. Nevertheless, there is no general agreement on which elicitation technique is the best, but there is a consensus that selecting an appropriate elicitation technique greatly affects the success or failure of the requirements elicitation process [32,54].

Requirements classification is the activity that takes an unstructured collection of requirements and groups them into coherent clusters [70]. Requirements can be classified in many different ways [5], yet they can be broadly classified under functional and non-functional requirements, where the first type refers to functionalities that the system shall deliver, and the second type refers to how the system shall deliver such functionalities [13]. More specifically, non-functional requirements are generic qualitative properties of the system as a whole, i.e., they refer to properties of the overall system, such as reliability, usability, supportability, etc. [42]. Moreover, functional requirements have clear-cut criteria for their satisfaction, while non-functional requirements can rarely be said to be accomplished or "satisfied" in a clear-cut sense [53]. Concerning security and privacy several different classifications have been proposed in the literature. For example, Singhal and Wijesekera [67] propose an ontology to classify security needs in terms of *threats, attacks, vulnerabilities, risks,* and *security mechanisms*. While [76] proposed to represent security needs using the following concepts: *assets, vulnerabilities, threats, countermeasures,* and *security policy*. Kang and Liang [38] classify security concerns into: *auditing, threats, accountability, non-repudiation, risk, attacks, availability, frauds, confidentiality, asset, integrity, prevention,* and *reputation*. On the other hand, Labda et al. [41] classify privacy needs in terms of *access control, Separation of Tasks (SoT), Binding of Tasks (BoT), user consent,* and *Necessity to know (NtK)*. In [37] *privacy goals* were classified under eight types namely, *authentication, authorization, identification, data protection, anonymity, pseydonymity, unlinkability,* and *unobservability.* While Solove [68] provides taxonomy for classifying privacy related problems under four main groups of possible harmful activities: *information collection, information processing, information dissemination,* and *information invasion.* Finally, other types of classifications have been proposed to sub-classify requirements such as risk [50], trust [82], information quality [23], etc.

Requirements prioritization is the activity to classify requirements on the base of their importance [30, 70], which enables for making decisions on which requirements should be implemented by the system-to-be. According to Berander and Andrews [51], prioritizing requirements allows for: deciding the core requirements of the system; selecting an optimal set requirements to be implemented, i.e., selecting a subset of requirements to realize a system that satisfies stakeholders' needs; estimating the expected users' satisfaction; and balancing the benefits of each requirement against the costs for its implementation. Several techniques for requirements prioritization has been already proposed in literature, such as: *Analytic Hierarchy Process (AHP),* in which decision makers pair-wise compare the requirements to determine which of the two is more important [39]; *cumulative voting (the 100 point method),* in which each stakeholder is given 100 points that he/she can use for voting in favor of the most important requirements [44]; *Bubblesort,* one of the simplest prioritization methods that sort requirements according to their priorities [39]; *ranking* [39], in which requirements are ranked based on their importance starting from the most important requirement until reaching the least important ones; *Top-Ten requirements* [42], in which stakeholders are asked to choose top-ten requirements out of all the requirements set without assigning an internal order between the requirements; or *numerical assignment (grouping)* [51], which is one of the most common prioritization technique that groups requirements into different priority groups based on their importance (e.g. critical, standard, and optional).

Requirements validation is concerned with showing that the set of requirements define the system that the stakeholders expect [40, 70]. Requirements validation is very important since detecting errors in the requirements during the design phase is much less expensive and time-consuming than discovering such errors after the system implementation [52]. One of the most well known method for requirements validation is presented in [70], which suggests five checks to be performed on the requirements: (1) *validity check* aiming at verifying the requirements with all relevant stakeholders for the system-to-be; (2) *completeness check* aiming at verifying that t requirements capture all the system functionalities and features (e.g., properties, constraints, etc.) expected by the stakeholders; (3) *consistency check* aiming at verifying that there is no inconsistencies among all requirements, i.e., there is no requirement that conflicts with any other requirement; (4) *realism check* aiming at verifying that requirements can actually be implemented; (5) *verifiability check* aiming at verifying that stakeholders and contractor(s) have the exact same understanding of the elaborated requirements, so to reduce potential disputes between them. All requirements should be written in clear way so both parties can understand and agree on them.

3 A Holistic Approach for Privacy Requirements Analysis

In this section, we present the approach we used to analyse the privacy requirements for the VisiOn platform. Particularly, we give an overview of the main phases of the process which will be further detailed in the next section specifically in the context of the VisiOn project [26]. The approach follows of the four general requirements engineering activities introduced in Sect. 2 (i.e., requirements elicitation, classification, prioritization, and validation) and proposes a process consisting of six main interrelated activities Fig. 1.

1. Identifying the scope. Defining the scope of the project is, usually, the most appropriate way to start [62]. This is the first activity of our process aiming at determining the boundary of the system accordingly to the main objectives to be achieved [46]. In order to properly identify the scope, we have to collect as much as possible information related to the outcome of the system to be developed and its possible application domains along with its intended users. Moreover, this activity is essential for the appropriate allocation of the project resources, indeed identifying the scope correctly reduces wasting of resources and avoids unnecessary activities. The main outcome of this activity is a *system and domain analysis*.

2. Stakeholder analysis aims at identifying all stakeholders that may influence, or that can be influenced, by the system. Stakeholders are then classified in coherent groups so to generalize their needs and expectations. This activity mainly focus on the identification of two groups of stakeholders: stakeholders who own personal information (legitimate information owners) and stakeholders who deal with/manage such information. Both of these groups play main roles while eliciting, classifying, and prioritizing privacy requirements. This activity is composed of two sub-activities:

2.1 Stakeholder identification & classification take the *system and domain analysis* as input and identify an initial list of stakeholders, which is further analyzed to identify any other relevant stakeholder. Since an inadequate stakeholders identification leads to inadequate stakeholder analysis [45], an accurate list of all possible stakeholders has to be produced at this stage. Then, identified stakeholders are further grouped into coherent groups[1] to better communicate with them, learn about their needs, integrate them into RE activities (e.g., in the requirements consolidation activity), and prioritizing their needs accordingly to their importance [45].

---

[1] These groups are not mutually exclusive, i.e., a stakeholder may belong to all of them.

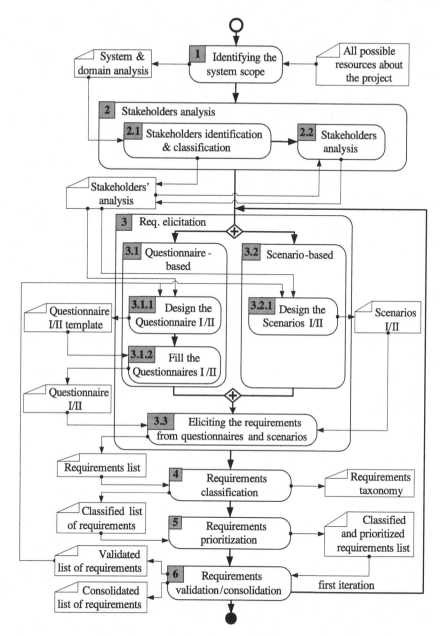

Fig. 1. The process for the specification of privacy requirements

2.2 Stakeholder analysis aims at analyzing each single stakeholder that has been identified in terms of its needs and expectations. We use Socio Technical Security - modelling language (STS-ml) [55], a goal based modeling language, to represent and analyze stakeholders and their objectives. We restricted the choice to goal-based modeling languages because they allow for an explicit representation of stakeholders' objectives and their needs. In particular, we selected STS-ml because it allows for a clear representation of stakeholders' objectives and their relation.

3. Requirements elicitation. Once stakeholders are identified, the process of requirements elicitation begins. The elicitation process is all about determining stakeholders' needs and it is performed incrementally and iteratively adding details about requirements [83]. Adopting the right elicitation technique from existing ones (e.g., interviews, questionnaires, task analysis, scenarios, prototyping, etc.) greatly affects the success of the requirements elicitation process [32,54]. Moreover, many projects adopt more than one technique for requirements elicitation [33,83] to improve the reliability and quality of elicited requirements. In this context, we have adopted two different techniques, namely *questionnaire-based* and *scenario-based*. These two techniques complement each other: the former has been adopted because it allows for collecting multiple stakeholders' requirements simultaneously, eliciting the actual stakeholders' requirements, and most importantly its flexibility in contacting the stakeholders; the latter has been chosen because it allows for interactively involving stakeholders during the requirements elicitation process, which is essential for privacy requirements due to the vague nature of such requirements [24]. The requirements elicitation activity is repeated twice, with the main purpose of eliciting more detailed privacy requirements in the second iteration and it is composed of three main sub-activities:

3.1 Questionnaire-based requirements elicitation. This activity is composed of two main activities *3.1.1 Design the questionnaire* and *3.1.2 Filling the questionnaire*, where the first aims at designing the questionnaire template and the last aims at sharing the questionnaires with the stakeholders and receive their feedback. In the first iteration, the first questionnaire is designed and filled by stakeholders, while in the second iteration, the questionnaires is refined in more detailed questions accordingly to the feedback collected in the first iteration and filled again by stakeholders.

3.2 Scenario-based requirements elicitation. This activity aims at defining several scenarios where personal information become critical for stakeholders. They are defined by stakeholders assisted by the analyst responsible of the requirements elicitation activity. Each scenario is then used to elicit stakeholders' privacy requirements. Similar to activity 3.1, this activity is repeated twice, where scenarios I and scenarios II are modeled in the first and second iteration of the activity, respectively.

3.3 Extracting privacy requirements. In this activity, the analyst extracts requirements from questionnaires and scenarios and integrate them in a consistent and coherent list. Practically, the analyst identifies explicit and implicit requirements from the answers of stakeholders and their expectations highlighted in the scenarios. Duplicated requirements are eliminated and conflictual situations are solved.

4. Requirements classification. Relying on existing requirements taxonomies, this activity aims at classifying requirements into coherent groups with closely related characteristics. When existing taxonomies do not cover types for some requirement, new classifications/sub-classifications are introduced. A taxonomy can reduce or remove any vagueness while dealing with requirements, and in turn, it contributes to better understanding of how requirements can be realized. Note that, the two stakeholders groups, namely information owners and who manage personal information, should be actively involved in this activity; particularly while extending the taxonomy to cover the privacy related concerns. In summary, this activity takes the requirements list and relays on existing requirement taxonomies to classify them accordingly. The taxonomy is refined iteratively with the active participation of stakeholders until it covers all types of requirements. After that, each requirement is assigned to a classification/sub-classification, the list of classified requirements is shared with all stakeholders so to receive their feedback and possibly revise further the taxonomy.

5. Requirements prioritization aims at prioritizing requirements based on their importance. Requirements should be prioritized mainly on the base of stakeholders' suggestions. Different weights can be associated to different groups of stakeholders so to reflect the importance and relevance of their feedback [45] and allowing for more accurate prioritization. In addition, the prioritization process should also consider requirements interdependencies that are largely [31]. Considering requirements interdependencies enable for better decisions concerning requirements implementation. For instance, a requirement might be classified as a low priority based on the feedback of the stakeholders (might not be implemented), yet it is *required* by a high priority requirement(s) (should be implemented). In such case, the latter requirement cannot be achieved without implementing the former one, therefore, such requirement should be implemented even it has been classified as a low priority requirement by the stakeholders.

6. Requirements validation/consolidation aims at verifying that the list of requirements captures all functionalities and qualities required by the stakeholders, the requirements are consistent one another, and a real-world solution can be used to implement each of these requirements [70, 74]. Our approach adopts the validation method proposed in [70], which performs five checks to validate the requirements, namely, *validity, completeness, consistency, realism,* and *verifiability* checks. On the other hand, requirements consolidation is the final activity of the process and it replicates the same activities performed during the validation, but in a more binding way since it produces the final list of requirements, i.e., no more modification or refinement for any of the requirements will be further performed.

4 Analyzing Privacy Requirements for the VisiOn Platform

This section gives a detailed description of how we applied our approach to analyzing the VisiOn stakeholders' privacy requirements. The process follows what has been proposed in the previous section and illustrated in Fig. 1 and consists of five main interrelated activities (classification, prioritization and validation the VisiOn requirements are combined in one single activity). In the rest of this section, we describe each of these activities.

1. Identifying the VisiOn project scope. In order to get a better understanding the overall scope of the VisiOn project, we depended on the VisiOn proposal and all available documentations that have been obtained from the partners[2] as input to analyze the scope of the VisiOn project. This activity produced the *VisiOn project & domain analysis*, which is used for the *VisiOn stakeholders analysis* activity.

2. VisiOn stakeholders analysis. This section summarizes our activities for identifying, classifying and analyzing the stakeholders of the VisiOn platform.

2.1 Stakeholders identification & classification. Depending on the *VisiOn project & domain analysis*, all identified stakeholders can be described as: stakeholders who represent legitimate owners of personal information), stakeholders who deal with/manage personal information, or stakeholders who are responsible for providing components for the VisiOn Privacy Platform (VPP) – VPP will be developed by integrating the partners existing software and tools. Therefore, we classify the stakeholders into three main groups (roles): *(1) Citizen*, people that will use VisiOn to define, visualize and control how their personal information are used by others (e.g., PAs); *(2) PA*, organizations that will use VisiOn to visualize, manage and control how the citizens' personal information are used and for which reasons by their own services and those provided by others[3]; and *(3) Component provider*, representing a VisiOn's partner that provides technical components for the final VisiOn platform. They contributed with requirements of each component and information of the integration among the components of the VPP.

2.2 Stakeholders analysis. After identifying the three main types of VPP stakeholders, we analyzed each of them in terms of their objectives related to the VisiOn's scope. Figure 2 shows the main stakeholder types along with their objectives represented with STS-ml [55]. STS-ml is a modeling language focused on social/organizational interactions between entities in socio-technical systems, i.e., systems where humans and technical components interact with each other to achieve common objectives. PA systems are an example of socio-technical systems: they are composed of technical components, such as the software services use to manage fees or payment, and humans, such as the citizens and the employees of the PAs. In STS-ml, autonomous entities (both humans and technological components) are called *actors*. Actors can be specified in an STS-ml diagram as *roles*, to represent a set of autonomous entities, or as *agents*, to represent a specific entity. For example, "Citizen" is considered a role, because it represents the set of people in a given country,

---

[2] Partners refer to the full consortium of the VisiOn project.
[3] Citizens and PAs roles can be generalized to a User stakeholder role.

while "George" is considered an agent since it is a single person. Roles are graphically represented with a pink solid circle, with a half circle in the lower part, while agents are represented with the same solid pink circle but with a segment in the upper part. Objectives that a stakeholder aims to achieve, are called *Goals* and are graphically represented as green solid ovals. Examples of goals are "PA trusted", which consists in building confidence in PA, or "software provided", which consists in providing software tools. The oval shapes attached to actors represent their *scopes*: the set of goals positioned inside a scope is assigned to the actor and specifies that the actor is in charge for fulfilling them. For example, in Fig. 2 *Citizen* is in charge of the goal *PA trusted*. Goals can be refined through "and-decomposed" or "or-decomposed" into subgoals, where in and-decomposition all subgoals must be achieved to fulfill the main goal, while only one of the subgoals must be achieved to fulfill the main goal in the or-decomposition. Figure 2 shows the objectives of stakeholders. Citizens have the main objective of trusting the PA. This goal can be split in three subgoals that must be reached in order to trust the PA that are: *Privacy issues shown, Consent managed* and *Sensitive data protected*. The first goal is and-decomposed in two subgoals: *show privacy violation*, which consists in promptly receiving information about violation of privacy in PA's systems, and *threats visualized*, which consists in receiving information from the PA about the threat to privacy on citizens information. *Consent managed* goal consists in reading and signing consents, while *Sensitive data protected* is and-decomposed in tree sub-goals: *Privacy req. specified, Privacy req. Visualized* and *Privacy req. enforced*. The three goals are achieved respectively if citizens' requirements are specified by the citizens and PA, shown by the PA to the citizens and enforced in PA system.

3. (I) Eliciting the VisiOn requirements (first iteration). In what follows, we describe the activities we performed to elicit VisiOn user requirements during the first iteration.

3.1 (I) VisiOn Requirements Questionnaire I. Contains two sub-activities that describe how the first VisiOn requirements questionnaire was designed and filled by the partners respectively.

    3.1.1 (I) Designing the VisiOn Questionnaire I (Q1). The requirements for building a system can be elicited from several sources [48], including stakeholders, users, documentation, and other existing systems [83]. Therefore, the first VisiOn Questionnaire template was designed to elicit requirements from the following three main sources: *(1) application domains,* which should be explored together with its political, organizational, social aspects, constraints that may influence the system [35,83]; *(2) stakeholders,* are the entities who can influence, or are being influenced by the system, where analyzing the stakeholders of the system is a key factor for the success of the overall requirements elicitation process [8]; and *(3) intended users,* are the entities who directly interact with the system to

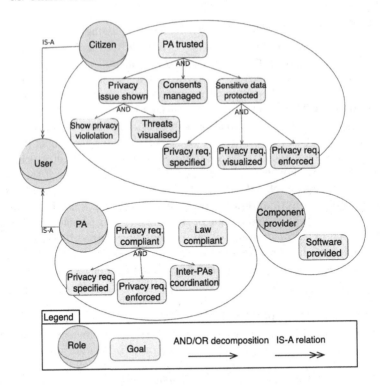

Fig. 2. Objectives of stakeholders of VisiOn

perform their work, and they play a central role in the requirements elicitation process as some requirements can be defined only by them (e.g.,
usability, supportability) [54]. In this context, the questionnaire contains
four main sections to be filled by the partners concerning: *(1) application
domains, (2) stakeholders*[4]*, (3) intended users,* and *(4) examples of usage*
that identify at least three possible scenarios in the application domains,
where users may use the VisiOn platform. This may reveal new requirements that the partner forgets to mention while compiling the previous
sections.

3.1.2 (I) Filling and refining the VisiOn Questionnaire I (Q1). The questionnaire template has been shared with four End-User (E-U) partners that
represent both PAs and citizens, and we asked them to fill and return. Few
days after sharing the questionnaire, the partners started contacting us
asking for some clarifications about some concerns related to their input.
We have answered each of the raised concerns, and support them with
more information when it is required. Once we received the filled questionnaires, we analyzed them appropriately adding our comments wherever

---

[4] To extend our knowledge about the stakeholders analysis (activity 2), and uncover
any stakeholder that has not been identified so far.

a clarification is needed from the partner. In several cases, we supported our comments with general examples to assist the partner in replying to them. And then, we sent back the questionnaire to the partners to refine their input. In some cases, the questionnaire was sent back and forth to the partner several times until their input is clear and understandable. The returned questionnaires were carefully analyzed, and we have identified 32 stakeholders and 12 users of VPP along with their objectives, excepted functionalities and qualities.

3.2 (I) Modeling and analyzing the scenarios I. The consortium of the VisiOn project is composed by two type of partners: technical partners, who provide the software and create the VisiOn platform, and the pilot partners, who are PAs and use their premises to evaluate and validate the platform. The pilot partners are one Spanish hospital, one Italian hospital, one Italian ministry and one Greek company who manage the municipality of Athens services. In this chapter, we use the latter as a running example, we did not include the other case studies for space limit. During the initial part of the VisiOn project, we asked the Pilot partners to define at least three scenarios each, where the management of personal information is critical, in terms of privacy, for both Citizens and PAs. We asked them to use STS-ml [55] for modeling these scenarios. STS-ml requirements models are created by the construction of three complementary views:

- **The social view** (shown in Fig. 3) is built on three concepts: *actor* that can be divided into a *role* (e.g., *Citizen*) or an *agent* (e.g., *Management system*), *goal* (e.g., "Birth certificate obtained"), and *document* that is a tangible supporting materials (e.g., "Birth certificate"). A goal may *produce* a document, i.e., the document is created when the goal is achieved (e.g., "Birth certificate issued" will *produces* the document "Birth certificate"). It may *read* a document, i.e., the actor linked to the goal needs to read the document in order to achieve the goal (e.g.., the actor "Citizen" needs to read the "Birth certificate" to achieve the goal "Birth certificate obtained"). An actor can also *modify* a document to achieve a goal. The interactions between actors are represented with two relations, *transmission* and *delegation*. The former represents the *transmission* of a document between two actors. For example, in Fig. 3 "Citizen" *transmits* the "ID copy" to "Citizen Registry". *Delegation* of a goal represents the assignment of an objective from an actor to another actor, i.e., with a delegation the responsibility of achieving a goal in transferred to another actor. For example, in Fig. 3 "Citizen" *delegates* the goal of "Birth certificate issued" to "Citizen Registry". STS-ml permits to specify security and privacy requirements on *transmissions* and *delegations*. For example, Fig. 3 three of them are shown: *integrity*, represented with a "Int" string inside a pink box, *confidentiality*, represented with a "Con" string inside a brown box, and *authentication*, represented with a "Auth" string inside a yellow box. *Integrity* can be specified on *transmissions* and it means that the document received is the same as the document sent. *Confidentiality*

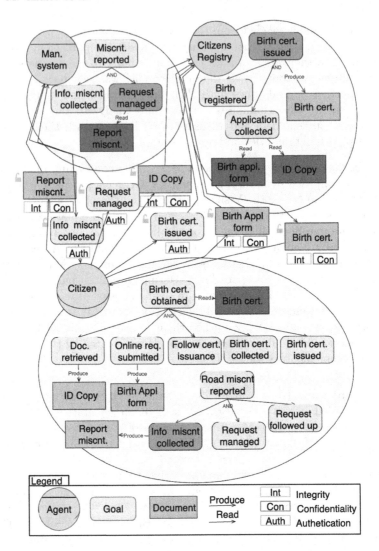

Fig. 3. STS-ml social view (Color figure online)

is specified on *transmissions* and it means that only authorized users can read the document that is sent. *Authentication* can be specified on *delegations*, and indicates that the source and destination actors must prove their identity, e.g., using an authentication security mechanism.

- **The information view** (shown in Fig. 5) is built on two concepts: *document* and *information*. The latter represents intangible data, such as name, surname, bank account details that is stored in one or more document. The relation *Tangible By* connects an *information* to a *document* and specifies that the information is stored in that document. For example, in Fig. 5 information

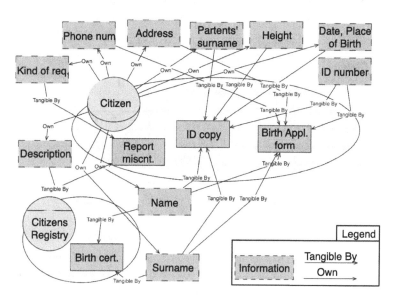

Fig. 4. STS-ml authorization view

"Name" that is stored in "Birth certificate". Information can be possessed by at most one actor. This is represented with the *Own* relation that connects an actor to an information and specifies that the actor is the legitimate owner of information. For example, in Fig. 5 the "Citizen" role *own* information "Name".

- **The authorization view** (shown in Fig. 4) is used to represent the authorizations that actors grant to one another over their information. The authorization relation connects two actors and it consists of three parts: (i) a set of authorizations, i.e., **R**ead, **M**odify, **P**roduce and **T**ransmit; (ii) a set of information, i.e., the target of the authorizations; and (iii) the scope of the authorization, i.e., the sot of goals for which the authorization is granted. For example, in Fig. 4 the authorization relation between *Citizen* and *Management system* authorizes the latter to read and transmit "Picture", "Description", "Location details" and "Kind of request" information. Since the scope part is empty, the authorization does not specify any constraint for what concerns the scope. Each partner was assisted by a modeling expert while modeling its scenarios. The models have been refined iteratively through several modeling sessions. The resulting models were analyzed by STS-tool [66], a software framework which supports STS-ml, to detect any modeling deficiencies and inconsistencies. Once they were verified, they were used to generate VisiOn user requirements. This feature of the tool automatically derives requirements form the models, based on the goals, the dependencies and interaction between actors and security constraints defined is the diagrams.

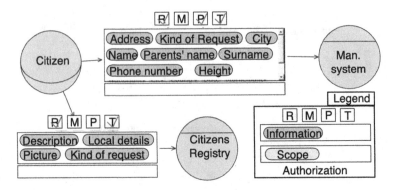

Fig. 5. STS-ml information view

3.3 (I) Eliciting the VisiOn requirements from questionnaires I and scenarios I.
Once all the questionnaires are filled and refined, and all the scenarios are
modeled and analyzed, we have used them to elicit the stakeholders' needs. In
summary, 91 stakeholders' needs were elicited, where these needs have been
used to elaborate the first set of the VisiOn user requirements (99 requirements). In particular, when the stakeholder's need is clear enough, it is considered as a requirement. While when the need is not clear, it is refined into a
requirement or more. Note that adopting two different techniques for requirements elicitation, significantly improved the quality of the requirements we
elicited. For example, the same requirement might be elicited by the two techniques, yet it is unlikely that both techniques elicit the exact same requirement. Therefore, the two versions of the requirement can be used to produce
more detailed requirement. In addition, we assigned different groups to perform the two elicitation techniques in order to reduce the impact that one
technique might have on the other, and in turn, might influence the quality
of the elicited requirements. Finally, each of the identified needs and requirements has been assigned a unique identifier that specifies the source where
the requirement has been first identified. This is particularly important for
requirements traceability reasons, i.e., it enables for tracing requirements back
to their original sources and identify what kind of modifications have been
applied to them. The list of VisiOn requirements has been shared with the
partners to receive their feedback, which we took into account while revising
the requirements.

4. Classifying, Prioritizing and Validating the VisiOn requirements.
This section describes how we classify, prioritize and validate the VisiOn requirements elicited during the first iteration of the requirements elicitation activity.

- *Design the VisiOn requirements classification, prioritization and validation
  questionnaire.* The questionnaire presents a table that contains the elicited
  requirements, where each requirement has been assigned a *type* based on our

proposed classification, a *priority* of the requirement to be filled by the partner (1 low - 5 high), and a text box to add any *comment/suggestion* concerning the requirement. In particular, 17 individuals from nine different partners have participated in this activity, and we asked them to analyze the table, to provide priorities, to check the classification/sub-classification we assigned to the requirements and revise if needed. Moreover, we provided them with a table that contains a *mapping* between the requirements and the VisiOn components that will realize them, and we asked them to provide feedback. This section has been added to help component developers to understand better their responsibilities, and how they should extend their component(s) to realize the requirements. Moreover, it facilitates performing the *requirements realism check*[5]. In addition, we ask them to check the requirement carefully and, possibly, to extend the list with other relevant requirements if required.

- *VisiOn requirements classification.* As previously mentioned, RE community broadly classifies requirements under functional and non-functional requirements, where the first have clear-cut criteria for their satisfaction, and the last do not have such criteria [13,53,70]. In this context, we proposed a taxonomy that differentiates between two main types of requirements, functional and non-functional requirements. More specifically, when the requirements have clear-cut criteria for their satisfaction, they are classified as functional requirements; otherwise, they are classified as non-functional requirements. In addition, we provide a classification/sub-classification for both functional and non-functional requirements based on the related literature to covers all types of the elicited requirements. In particular, non-functional requirements have been further sub-classified under four types, namely usability, reliability, performance, and supportability [53]. Functional requirements were further sub-classified under four types of requirements namely, privacy requirements, security requirements, IQ requirements and trust requirements. Since no existing work proposes a well-defined taxonomy to classify privacy requirements, they have been classified based on the common aspects of privacy identified based on the feedback we received from the stakeholders taking into consideration the five components of VisiOn Platform[6] (privacy assessment, privacy requirements, privacy specification, privacy run-time, and privacy transparency visualization). To this end, *privacy requirements* have six main sub-categories, 1- information ownership, 2- information control (authentication), 3- information usage, 4- information transmission, 5- privacy assessment, and 6- privacy verification.

- *Security requirements* have been considered to capture the main stakeholders' security concerns. In our taxonomy, security requirements have six main sub-categories that have been chosen based on the best practices concerning capturing security requirements in the literature [50,52,73,82], namely 1- confidentiality, 2- integrity, 3- availability, 4- vulnerability, 5- threat, and 6- attack. While *Trust requirements* have been considered to capture the actors'

---

[5] Requirements realism will be discussed later in this section.

[6] Next chapters provide more information about VisiOn components.

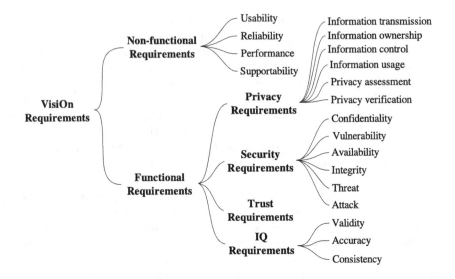

Fig. 6. VisiOn requirements taxonomy

expectations in one another concerning their objectives and dependencies [52,82]. Finally, *IQ requirements* [10,23] have been considered to address stakeholders' needs concerning information accuracy, validity, and consistency. Therefore, IQ requirements have three main sub-categories, 1- accuracy, 2-validity, and 3- consistency. Once the taxonomy is considered complete, i.e., it covers all types of VisiOn requirements, we provide the partners with a table that contains the list of requirements, which have been assigned types based on our proposed classification, and we asked them to provide feedback. The returned feedback was carefully examined while producing the final taxonomy of the VisiOn requirements that is depicted in Fig. 6.

- *VisiOn requirements prioritization.* Requirements prioritization is the process of classifying the requirements based on their importance [30,70], which enables system developers to make decisions on which requirements should be implemented. Among the existing requirements prioritizing techniques (e.g., Analytic Hierarchy Process (AHP), Cumulative Voting, Ranking), we have adopted the numerical assignment (grouping) [51], which is the most common prioritization technique and it is standardized (see IEEE Std. 830-1998 [15]). In the numerical assignment, requirements are classified into different priority groups based on their importance (e.g. critical, standard, and optional). In particular, we asked the partners to prioritize each of the requirements on an ordinal scale from 1–5, where 1 is the least important and 5 is the most important. After that, we classified the partners based on their role in the VisiOn project under End-Users (E-U) (i.e., Citizens and/or PAs), System Integrators (SID) and Research and Academic (R-C). Then we calculated the requirements priority value for each of three partners' types. This was followed by assigning qualitative values instead of the numbered ones to enable qualitative reasoning concerning requirements prioritization. In particular, priority is **High** if its priority is at least four, it is **Medium** if its priority is at least three and less than four, and the priority is **Low** if it is less than three. Furthermore, following [59], we assigned different weights to the input received from the different partners' categories. More specifically, the input received from E-U partners was considered as the most relevant since they represent the actual users of VPP (Citizens and PAs), followed by the SID partners input since they have experience in developing and commercializing software products, while the least important is the R-C partners input since they have experience in developing software products. Table 1 shows how we determine the priority of the requirements based on the input from the different partners. The priority values are evaluated qualitatively as follows: we have priority **H** when the priority expressed by E-U is **H**, while both of the priority values expressed by SID and R-C are at least **M**. The priority value is **M** if it was expressed by E-U as **M**, and both of the priority values expressed by SID and R-C are at least **M**. Finally, the priority is **L** if the priority expressed by E-U is **L** regardless of the input provided by SID and R-C, or when the priority expressed by E-U is **M**, and at least one of the SID and R-C has expressed it **L**. On the other hand, requirement dependency is gaining more attention in requirements prioritization lately [31,51,63]. According to Carlshamre et al. [11] only fifth of the requirements are not related to or influenced by other requirements. Therefore, the final decision concerning requirements implementation should not only depend on their assigned priorities, but also on its relation(s) with other requirements. Following [11], we have considered three different relations among requirements:

- *Requires,* which implies that the fulfillment of one requirement depends on the fulfillment of another one. Usually, such relation is used to describe that if one requirement is to be included into the system, it requires another requirement to be included as well, i.e., a requirement is a prerequisite or pre-condition for another one. For example, if one requirement states that the system should include web-access, a network connection is required.
- *Conflicts_with,* which means that a requirement is in conflict with another one, if they cannot exist at the same time, i.e., fulfilling one of them decreases or even prevent the fulfillment of the other. For example, if one requirement states that the system should include web-access, and another one state that no access to the system should be allowed from the web, we say that these two requirements are conflicting, i.e., the system will not be able to fulfill both of them.

Table 1. Priority matrix

Priority	H	M	M	M	L	L	L
E-U	H	M	H	H	L	M	M
SID	M	M	L	–	–	L	–
R-C	M	M	–	L	–	–	L

ID	Requirement Description	Requires	Increases/Decreases value of
1	The VisiOn platform shall provide user-friendly interfaces for its users.	-	[+] 9,10,11,12,16,21, 33,49,50,67
2	The VisiOn platform shall support access to the citizen's information to authorized users only.	3,6,32,76	-
3	The VisiOn platform shall analyse the users' authorizations based on their needs to perform their activities.	69	-
4	The VisiOn platform shall control the usage of its services to authorised users' only.	-	-

Fig. 7. A Snapshot of the relations among the VisiOn requirements

– *Increases/Decreases_value_of,* occurs when choosing one requirement for implementation increases or decreases the value to the customer of another requirement(s), i.e., implementing a specific requirement may have a positive or negative influence on the customer value of some requirements. For example, providing a context-dependent notification system to the software will increase the customer satisfaction, since the software will automatically modify the notification means without any involvement at the customer side when the context changes.

Figure 7, shows a snapshot of the table that captures the relations among the VisiOn requirements[7]. Identifying such relations is essential to specify how some requirements are essential for the satisfaction of other ones and how some requirements add value to other ones, which helps in deciding which requirements should be implemented. In other words, considering requirement dependencies enables for avoiding situations where some requirements have been classified as low priority based on the feedback of the stakeholders, and they are *required by/increases_value_of* high priority requirements.

• *VisiOn requirements validation.* The first elicited set of VisiOn requirements was validated by the feedback received from the partners and the individual

---

[7] Conflicts_with relations are not shown in the table since we already resolve all the inconsistencies that use to exist among the requirements.

meetings we arrange with them during the Technical Meeting[8]. In Particular, we ask them to check the requirement carefully and provide a feedback concerning them.

5. (II) Eliciting the VisiOn User Requirements (second iteration). This section describes our activities for eliciting the VisiOn user requirements during the second iteration of this activity.

5.1(II) VisiOn Requirements Questionnaire II. In what follows, we describe how the second VisiOn requirements questionnaire II was designed and filled.

5.1.1 (II) Design the VisiOn Questionnaire II (Q2). Q2 was designed with the main objective of eliciting more detailed requirements from the two types of VisiOn users (PA and citizen) concerning their functionalites and qualities, how they are expected to interact with VisiOn to perform such functionalities, and how the platform is expected to realize their defined qualities. In addition, Q2 was designed in a way to link the users' feedback with the different components of the VPP, which enable the component developers to better understand how they can modify and extend their tools/components to meet the defined functionalities and qualities. Therefore, we provided a specialized version of the questionnaire for each partner taking into consideration his/her input in Q1. In particular, Q2 template includes two sub-questionnaires specialized for the two types of VisiOn users (PA and citizen), to be filled by the partner for each PA and citizen users identified by them in Q1. In what follows, we describe each of the sub-questionnaire. Each of these sub-questionnaire contains six sections. The first section is different between the two sub-questionnaires, in the *PA user questionnaire* it aims to describe the *(1) system analysis,* that captures the interaction between the VPP and the system(s) that is/are using the citizens' information, and in the *citizen user questionnaire* it aims to describe the *(1) privacy requirements - identification,* that captures how the citizen is expected to interact with the VPP to specify its privacy requirements and how the VPP is expected to assist him/her during the process, etc. While the two questionnaires share the same following five sections, *(2) privacy requirements - visualization,* to capture what kind of information a PA/citizen might need to visualize, how it needs to visualize it, etc.; *(3) privacy requirements analysis,* to capture what kind of analysis the VPP should provide, what is the expected output of such analysis, etc.; *(4) privacy requirements analysis at run-time,* to capture what kind of analysis the VPP should perform at run-time, what is the expected output for such analysis, etc.; *(5) Privacy Level Agreement (PLA),* to capture the PA/citizen expectations about the PLA, which enable us to extend our knowledge concerning the PA/citizen objectives; and *(6) examples of usage,* to elicit requirements of the PA/citizen that the partner might forget to mention while compiling the previous sections.

---

[8] Occurred in Rome with the participation of all VisiOn partners.

5.1.2 (II) Filling and refining the VisiOn Questionnaire II (Q2). In line with what we did for Q1, we shared Q2 with three E-U partners and we asked them to fill and return. Similar to the Q1 filling and refining process, we assist them during this process. After receiving the filled questionnaires, we analyzed them, and we contacted some partners to refine their input until it is clear. In summary, very detailed needs of six PAs and three Citizens concerning the VPP were identified.

5.2 (II) Modeling and Analyzing the Scenarios II. Similar to what we did in the first iteration of this activity, we asked the VisiOn partners to enrich the STS-ml models of the scenarios they created in the previous iteration. We organized a workshop, which lasted a day, in which one expert modeler and two domain experts, per pilot partner, analyzed and extended the previously created STS-ml models. After the workshop the domain experts kept updating the diagrams without the help of the modeling experts. This led to the creation of more complete models that cover, with great details, the scenarios. We used such models to identify the related VisiOn user requirements, on the part of the system included in the scenarios.

5.3 (II) Eliciting the VisiOn user requirements from questionnaires II and scenarios II. Similar to the first iteration of this activity, we used both of the questionnaires and scenarios to elicit the second set of VisiOn user requirements, which have been used to refine and extend the already elicited requirements to produce the final list of VisiOn user requirements (41 new requirements).

6. Consolidating the VisiOn requirements[9]. Requirements validation is very important activity, since detecting errors in the requirements during the design phase is much less expensive and time-consuming than discovering such errors after the system implementation [52]. Following [70], we performed five checks (validity, completeness, consistency, realism, and verifiability) to validate the VisiOn requirements. In what follows, we discuss how each of these checks has been performed to produce the final consolidated list of VisiOn requirements:

- *VisiOn requirements validity check,* aims to verify the elaborated requirements with all the stakeholders of the system-to-be. We performed this check by sharing the VisiOn requirements with all the partners, and we asked them to carefully check the requirements and provide us with their feedback. The feedback contains suggestions to revise and refine some requirements in order to better define the functionalities/features they require the system to deliver.
- *VisiOn requirements completeness check,* aims to verify that the elaborated requirements capture all the functions, features, constraints, etc. that are expected by the system users. We performed the completeness check by asking the End-User (E-U) partners that represent both PAs and citizens to check the elaborated list of requirements and whether they describe all the

---

[9] Requirements consolidation is used to refer to the validation of the final list of VisiOn user requirements.

ID	Requirement Description	Type	Source	Req. of PA/C	Comp onenet	Prio rity
1	The VisiOn platform shall provide user-friendly interfaces for its users.	NFR/ Usability	[OPBG _ST#2- 1-R1]	PA-C	PA, PV	H
2	The VisiOn platform shall support access to the citizen's information to authorized users only.	SR/ Confidenti ality	[OPBG _AD#2- 10-R1]	PA-C	PR, PS	H
3	The VisiOn platform shall analyse the users' authorizations based on their needs to perform their activities.	PR/ Info ownership	[OPBG _AD#2- 10-R1]	PA-C	PR, PS	H
ad ded	The VisiOn platform shall control the usage of its services to authorised users' only.	PR/ Info ownership	[OPBG _AD#2- 10-R1]	PA-C	PA, PV	H

Fig. 8. A snapshot of the requirements table shared with the partners

functionalities and features they expect the system to deliver. Some partners asked to add new requirements to the list that were not included in the requirements we elaborate.

- *VisiOn requirements consistency check,* aims to verify that the elaborated requirements are consistent with one another, i.e., no inconsistency should exist among them. The consistency check was able to detect some conflicts among the requirements. However, we manage to solve this issue by revising the conflicting requirements with the help of the partner(s) who identify such requirements[10].

- *VisiOn requirements realism check,* aims to verify that the requirements can actually be implemented. We performed this check by sharing the requirements list with the partners that are responsible for developing the components of the VPP, and we ask them to carefully check the requirements list and provide us with their feedback. The feedback contains suggestions to revise several requirements, and mark 15 of them as out of the VPP scope. In addition, we had teleconference meetings with them to discuss the requirements one-by-one. After the meeting, the requirements list was revised accordingly. A snapshot of the shared requirements table is shown in Fig. 8.

- *VisiOn requirements verifiability check,* aims to ensure that the requirements are documented in a clear and understandable way so that they can be verifiable by the different stakeholders of the system, which reduce any potential dispute among the stakeholders concerning the requirements. This check was performed by sharing the final list of requirements with End-Users (PAs and Citizens) and Component developers, i.e., both of them were able to check

---

[10] We depend on STS-ml to analyze the consistency of some of the functional requirements (e.g., security, trust, etc.).

and provide their feedback concerning the same requirements list. Both of them verify that the requirements are clear, understandable and describe all the functionalities and features they expect the system. Moreover, we kept records of all the documents we shared with the different partners along with their feedback on these documents, which enables for resolving any potential dispute between the two sides.

ID	Requirement Description	Type	Source	Req. of PA/C	Comp onenet	Prio rity
1	The VisiOn platform shall provide user-friendly interfaces for its users.	NFR/ Usability	[OPBG _ST#2-1-R1]	PA-C	PA, PV	H
2	The VisiOn platform shall support access to the citizen's information to authorized users only.	SR/ Confidenti ality	[OPBG _AD#2-10-R1]	PA-C	PR, PS	H
3	The VisiOn platform shall analyse the users' authorizations based on their needs to perform their activities.	PR/ Info ownership	[OPBG _AD#2-10-R1]	PA-C	PR, PS	H
4	The VisiOn platform shall control the usage of its services to authorised users' only.	PR/ Info ownership	[OPBG _AD#2-10-R1]	PA-C	PA, PV	H

Fig. 9. A Snapshot of the consolidated VisiOn user requirements

A snapshot of the table that contains the consolidated VisiOn user requirements is shown in Fig. 9, where each requirement is described with the following attributes:

- *Req. ID:* A unique identifier for each requirement.
- *Description:* a textual description of the requirement, and a clarificatory text for some requirement.
- *Type:* the type of the requirement based on our taxonomy.
- *Source:* used for traceability reasons, requirement source is represented with a unique identifier that specifies the source where the requirement has been elicited from.
- *Req. of (PA/C):* whether it is a requirement for Public Administration (PA) and/or for Citizen (C).
- *Component:* it identifies the component(s) that will realize such requirement, where we have five VisiOn components, Privacy Assessment (PA), Privacy Requirements (PR), Privacy Specification (PS), Privacy Run-Time (PRT), and Privacy Transparency Visualization (PTV).
- *Priority (H/M/L):* indicates how important the requirement is in order to achieve the objectives of the project: 1- (H)igh: Must have, 2- (M)edium: Should have, and 3- (L)ow: Nice to have.

5   Approach Threats to Validity

After presenting and discussing our approach, we discuss the threats to its validity. Following [79], we classify threats to validity under four types:

Threats to construct validity concerns the relationships between theory and observation, i.e., to what extent a test measures what it claims to be measuring [64, 79]. We have identified the following two threats: *(1) Hypothesis guessing,* occurs when a participant of the experiment is able to guess the desired result, which may influences his/her response [75]. To mitigate this threat, the different questionnaires concerning requirements elicitation, prioritization, classification and validation/consolidation were designed carefully in order not to influence nor guide the participants. *(2) Experimenter expectations,* occurs when experimenter's expectations are communicated unintentionally to participants [75]. To avoid such threat, we shared all the questionnaires with the partners who are not participants and ask them to check whether the questionnaire is properly designed, i.e., it does not communicate any information that might reveal the experiment expectations to the participants.

Threats to internal validity concerns with external factors that have not been considered in the study, and they could have influenced the dependent variables in the study [75]. We have identified one internal threat. *Researcher bias,* occurs when the researcher influences the outcome of the study. To reduce the probability of such threat, the role of the researchers during all the activities that involve participants were limited only to assist them when needed without influencing their decisions. Moreover, we followed clear criteria while dealing with the participants' feedback concerning requirements elicitation, prioritization, classification and validation/consolidation.

Threats to external validity concerns the ability to generalize the results of the study. We have identified the following external threat: *Extensive evaluation,* the approach has been applied to only one project that concerns different application areas. This may threaten *the generalization of our findings.* However, we aim to better validate the approach by applying it other projects in different application domains.

Threats to reliability validity concerns the relationship between the treatment and the outcome, i.e., to what extent the study is dependent on the researcher(s), i.e., if another researcher(s) conducted the same study, the result should be the same. Detailed information concerning all the performed activities/adopted techniques (e.g., questionnaires, scenarios) for eliciting, classifying, prioritizing and validating/consolidating the VisiOn requirements are available at [28], and the overall process can be repeated. However, repeating these activities may not return the exact same results, but it presents a strong evidence about the reliability of the approach application.

6   Related Work

Several approaches for Privacy Requirements Specification have been proposed in the literature. For instance, Spiekermann and Cranor [72] propose a framework that enables system analysts to build privacy friendly information systems. The framework contains high-level responsibilities for system analysts that stem from well-accepted definitions of privacy. In particular, according to the authors there are privacy issues in cases of data storage, transfer, and processing and the system analysts are instructed to understand privacy expectations of users. Four levels of system privacy friendliness are presented along with guidelines on how each level can be achieved. A basic principle of this approach is that the less easy is to identify a user based on some data the more privacy-friendly the system is.

A threat-based approach to elicit privacy requirements, named LINDDUN, is proposed by Deng et al. [16], which includes a systematic methodology and catalog of privacy related threat tree patterns. In particular, the authors propose a mapping of privacy threat types to system components that are modeled with Data Flow Diagrams (DFDs). Once privacy threat types are identified then they are further refined with the help of privacy threat tree patterns specifically developed for each threat type. Finally, the authors present a mapping of privacy requirements to existing Privacy Enhancing Technologys (PETs) in order to support analysts that are not experts in privacy technologies.

PriS [37] is a privacy requirements engineering method that allows system analysts to identify privacy requirements from the early stages of software development. Privacy requirements are considered organizational goals that must be satisfied by system under development. In particular, the method is based on the Enterprise Knowledge Development (EKD) framework where system requirements are modeled as goals and a goal hierarchy of the system is built. In turn, the analyst needs to identify processes that realize the goals. Similarly, privacy requirements are modeled as privacy goals, which may cause the modification of existing goals or the creation of new ones. Then, respective privacy processes have to be identified, which can be carried out with the support of a set of privacy-process patterns that the authors describe. Furthermore, appropriate privacy-enhancing technologies can be identified that support the business processes with regards to privacy.

The OASIS Privacy Management Reference Model and Methodology (PMRM) [65] focuses on the management of privacy requirements and risks. It contains a series of steps that guide analysts in the identification and scoping of use cases and mapping of privacy policies to privacy controls, both technical and procedural.

The PReparing Industry to Privacy-by-design by supporting its Application in REsearch (PRIPARE) methodology [60] is the result of a European Union funded project, which aims to integrate existing practices and research proposals on privacy engineering. It contains seven phases that enable the analyst to consider privacy issues, from the analysis phase where privacy requirements need to be identified to the decommission phase where personal data needs to be protected when the system is dismantled. During each phase, a number of different modeling languages and techniques are proposed for the analyst to employ, such as Unified Modelling Language (UML) or LINDDUN.

Radics et al. [58] present a framework that is mostly focused on the privacy requirements elicitation stage. In particular, it guides the analyst on the collection of relevant data that are used for the elicitation of privacy requirements through the identification of privacy related patterns in the collected data.

Some of the approaches reviewed above although they cover all the phases that are required for the specification of privacy requirements, they offer only high-level support to the analyst. On the other hand, there are approaches that include detailed steps for the completion of tasks but they do not cover all the tasks that are part of the privacy requirements specification. The approach that we employed in this chapter contained guidelines for all the required tasks, such as elicitation, classification, prioritization, and validation of privacy requirements.

General privacy taxonomies such as (Anton et al. [4]), (Solove et al. [68]), and (Wuyts et al. [80]) can serve as a general knowledge repository for a knowledge-based privacy goal refinement. However, they lack though a systematic process that can be followed in order to specify privacy requirements.

There are also approaches that consider privacy as part of security requirements. For example, Liu et al. [47] present a methodological framework that enables the identification of security and privacy requirements by employing a set of analysis mechanisms. These are applied within the i* modeling language, where security and privacy are considered as soft goals, and lead to the systematic extraction of security and privacy threats and related countermeasures.

Van Lamsweerde [77] present an extension of the KAOS framework for elaborating security requirements. In this method the software engineer constructs two models, an intentional model of the system under development and an anti-model that contains vulnerabilities and capabilities for achieving the anti-goals that threaten the systems security goals. Apart from confidentiality, integrity, availability, authentication, and non-repudiation, privacy is also considered as a security goal.

Giorgini et al. [27] introduce the concepts of ownership, provisioning, trust, and delegation, in order to enable software engineers to consider security issues throughout the whole development process. By employing the aforementioned concepts the authors claim that privacy requirements can be captured. Mouratidis and Giorgini [52] propose a security-oriented methodology is presented where a security requirement is considered as a restriction that can influence the analysis and design of a system under development by restricting some alternative design solutions, by conflicting with some of the requirements, or by refining the objectives of the system. Such restrictions can be in terms of integrity, availability, and privacy.

The above approaches treat privacy mainly as confidentiality protection of personal data. However, privacy goals include also anonymity, unlinkability, unobservability, and pseudonymity among others. Without appropriate techniques that force the software engineer to look at these aspects of privacy it is very likely that important privacy requirements will be omitted for the system under development.

7   Conclusions and Future Work

In this chapter, we have presented a holistic requirements engineering approach for eliciting, classifying, prioritizing and validating privacy requirements. In particular, it combines several existing requirements engineering activities that have been adapted in order to deal with privacy requirements. The approach has been successfully used to elicit, classify, prioritize and consolidate the VisiOn platform requirements. In particular, the consolidated list of requirements is the result of an iterative and incremental process that has intertwined the use of state of the art techniques for requirements elicitation with a close interaction with stakeholders and users, where these requirements have been used to define the main functionalities and qualities of two types of VPP users (e.g., PAs and citizens). In addition, the requirements have been used by component developers to identify how their tools need to be extended and integrated into the VPP. This approach has been developed to be used for real world projects (e.g., industry). Therefore, the process underlining the approach has been designed carefully to assist software engineers during the overall process for specifying privacy requirements. Moreover, each of the process activities has been accompanied with a detailed description of how it can be performed.

For future work, we are investigating how the proposed taxonomy of privacy requirements can be further refined into more concrete concepts depending on [25], and how privacy requirements are linked to other types of requirements such as security and trust. Moreover, we aim to better investigate the interdependencies between the requirements activities and especially between the two different requirements elicitation activities. In addition, we intend to provide a more expressive analysis of the mapping between requirements and the component of the system that will realize them. Finally, we aim to better validate the approach by applying it to other similar projects that belong to different domains.

Acronyms

PA	Public Administration
VPP	VisiOn Privacy Platform
RE	Requirements Engineering
AHP	Analytic Hierarchy Process
DFD	Data Flow Diagram
PET	Privacy Enhancing Technology
EKD	Enterprise Knowledge Development
PMRM	Privacy Management Reference Model and Methodology
PRIPARE	PReparing Industry to Privacy-by-design by supporting its Application in REsearch
UML	Unified Modelling Language
STS-ml	Socio Technical Security - modelling language

References

1. Acquisti, A., Friedman, A., Telang, R.: Is there a cost toprivacy breaches? An event study. In: 5th Workshop on the Economics of Information Security, pp. 1–20 (2006). https://doi.org/10.1.1.73.2942
2. Agarwal, R., Tanniru, M.R.: Knowledge acquisition using structured interviewing: an empirical investigation. J. Manage. Inf. Syst. **7**(1), 123–140 (1990). ISSN: 0742-1222. https://doi.org/10.1080/07421222.1990.11517884. http://www.tandfonline.com/doi/full/10.1080/07421222.1990.11517884
3. Antón, A.I., Earp, J.B., Reese, A.: Analyzing website privacy requirements using a privacy goal taxonomy. In: Proceedings of the IEEE International Conference on Requirements Engineering, vol. 2002, pp. 23–31. IEEE (2002). ISBN: 0769514650. https://doi.org/10.1109/ICRE.2002.1048502
4. Antn, A.I., Earp, J.B.: A requirements taxonomy for reducing Web site privacy vulnerabilities. Requir. Eng. **9**(3), 169–185 (2004). ISSN: 0947-3602. https://doi.org/10.1007/s00766-003-0183-z. http://link.springer.com/10.1007/s00766-003-0183-z
5. Aurum, A., Wohlin, C.: Requirements engineering: setting the context. In: Aurum, A., Wohlin, C. (eds.) Engineering and Managing Software Requirements, pp. 1–15. Springer, Heidelberg (2005). https://doi.org/10.1007/3-540-28244-0_1
6. Ball, L.J., Ormerod, T.C.: Putting ethnography to work: the case for a cognitive ethnography of design. Int. J. Hum. Comput. Stud. **53**(1), 147–168 (2000). ISSN: 10715819. https://doi.org/10.1006/ijhc.2000.0372. http://linkinghub.elsevier.com/retrieve/pii/S1071581900903720
7. Beckers, K., Pape, S.: A serious game for eliciting social engineering security requirements. In: Proceedings of the 2016 IEEE 24th International Conference on Requirements Engineering, RE 2016. IEEE, pp. 16–25 (2016). ISBN: 9781509041213. https://doi.org/10.1109/RE.2016.39
8. Belani, H., Pripuzic, K., Kobas, K.: Implementing web-surveys for software requirements elicitation. In: Proceedings of the 8th International Conference on Telecommunications, ConTEL 2005, pp. 465–469 (2005). ISBN: 953-184-081-4. https://doi.org/10.1109/CONTEL.2005.185931. http://ieeexplore.ieee.org/document/1458610/
9. Beyer, H.R., Holtzblatt, K.: Apprenticing with the customer. Commun. ACM **38**(5), 45–52 (1995). ISSN: 0001-0782. https://doi.org/10.1145/203356.203365. http://portal.acm.org/citation.cfm?doid=203356.203365
10. Bovee, M., Srivastava, R.P., Mak, B.: A conceptual framework and belief-function approach to assessing overall information quality. Int. J. Intell. Syst. **18**(1), 311–328 (2001). Paper presented at the Proceedings of the 6th International Conference on Information Quality
11. Carlshamre, P., et al.: An industrial survey of requirements interdependencies in software product release planning. In: Proceedings of the IEEE International Conference on Requirements Engineering, pp. 84–91. IEEE (2001). ISBN: 0-7695-1125-2. https://doi.org/10.1109/ISRE.2001.948547
12. Cavoukian, A.: Privacy by design: origins, meaning, and prospects. In: Privacy Protection Measures and Technologies in Business Organizations: Aspects and Standards: Aspects and Standards, p. 170 (2011)
13. Chung, L., et al.: Non-functional requirements in software engineering. In: Conceptual Modeling: Foundations and Applications, p. 472 (1999)
14. European Commission: European Data Protection Supervisor (2016). http://ec.europa.eu/justice/data-protection/bodies/supervisor/index_en.htm

15. IEEE Computer Society Software Engineering Standards Committee: Recommended practice for software requirements specifications. In: IEEE Std 830-1998. Institute of Electrical and Electronics Engineers (1998). ISBN: 0-7381-0332-2

16. Deng, M., et al.: A privacy threat analysis framework: supporting the elicitation and fulfillment of privacy requirements. Requir. Eng. **16**(1), 1–27 (2011). EBSCO. http://web.b.ebscohost.com.library.capella.edu/ehost/pdfviewer/pdfviewer? sid=e7ebe3bc-59f7-43a0-ace9-60485dc3acd3@sessionmgr111&vid=1&hid=118

17. Duncan, G.: Engineering privacy by design. Science (N.Y.) **317**(5842), 1178–1179 (2007). ISSN: 0036-8075. https://doi.org/10.1126/science.1143464

18. Ebrahim, Z., Irani, Z.: E-government adoption: architecture and barriers. Bus. Process Manage. J. **11**(5), 589–611 (2005)

19. Fernandes, J., et al.: iThink: a game-based approach towards improving collaboration and participation in requirement elicitation. Proc. Comput. Sci. **15**, 66–77 (2012). ISSN: 1877-0509. https://doi.org/10.1016/j.procs.2012.10.059. arXiv http://arxiv.org/abs/11/09. ACM (ISBN: 978-1-4503-0816-8)

20. Foddy, W.: Constructing Questions for Interviews and Surveys: Theory and Practice in Social Research. Cambridge University Press, Cambridge (1993). https://books.google.co.uk/books?hl=en&lr=&id=tok_OKwywQIC& oi=fnd&pg=PR7&dq=questionnaires+in+social+research&ots=Tybbm2R3LP& sig=Mqh2DafK5wKDOkcDuvOgIj3hl6s

21. Garlan, D., Allen, R., Ockerbloom, J.: Architectural mismatchor why it's hard to build systems out of existing parts. In: Proceedings of the 17th International Conference on Software Engineering, ICSE 1995, pp. 179–185. ACM (1995). ISBN: 0897917081. https://doi.org/10.1145/225014.225031. http://portal. acm.org/citation.cfm?doid=225014.225031

22. Gellman, R.: Privacy, Consumers, and Costs - How The Lack of Privacy Costs Consumers and Why Business Studies of Privacy Costs are Biased and Incomplete. Ford Foundation, pp. 1–37 (March 2002)

23. Gharib, M., Giorgini, P.: Modeling and reasoning about information quality requirements. In: Fricker, S.A., Schneider, K. (eds.) REFSQ 2015. LNCS, vol. 9013, pp. 49–64. Springer, Cham (2015). https://doi.org/10.1007/978-3-319-16101-3_4

24. Gharib, M., Giorgini, P., Mylopoulos, J.: Ontologies for Privacy Requirements Engineering: A Systematic Literature Review. arXiv preprint arXiv:1611.10097 (2016)

25. Gharib, M., Giorgini, P., Mylopoulos, J.: Towards an ontology for privacy requirements via a systematic literature review. In: Mayr, H.C., Guizzardi, G., Ma, H., Pastor, O. (eds.) ER 2017. LNCS, vol. 10650, pp. 193–208. Springer, Cham (2017). https://doi.org/10.1007/978-3-319-69904-2_16

26. Gharib, M., et al.: Privacy requirements: findings and lessons learned in developing a privacy platform. In: Proceedings of the 2016 IEEE 24th International Conference on Requirements Engineering, RE 2016, pp. 256–265. IEEE (2016). ISBN: 9781509041213. https://doi.org/10.1109/RE.2016.13

27. Giorgini, P., Massacci, F., Zannone, N.: Security and trust requirements engineering. In: Aldini, A., Gorrieri, R., Martinelli, F. (eds.) FOSAD 2004–2005. LNCS, vol. 3655, pp. 237–272. Springer, Heidelberg (2005). https://doi.org/10. 1007/11554578_8

28. Giorgini, P., et al.: D2.2 Citizens and public administration privacy requirements V 2.0. Technical report, Universitá degli studi di Trento (2016)

29. Goguen, J.A., Linde, C.: Techniques for requirements elicitation. In: 1993 Proceedings of the IEEE International Symposium on Requirements Engineering, vol. 93,

pp. 152–164 (1993). ISSN: 0740-7459. https://doi.org/10.1109/ISRE.1993.324822. http://ieeexplore.ieee.org/document/324822/

30. Helfert, M., Herrmann, C.: Proactive data quality management for data warehouse systems - a metadata based data quality system. In: 4th International Workshop on Design and Management of Data Warehouses, DMDW 2002, vol. 2002, pp. 97–106 (2002). http://sunsite.informatik.rwth-aachen.de/Publications/CEUR-WS/Vol-58/herrmann.pdf

31. Herrmann, A., Daneva, M.: Requirements prioritization based on benefit and cost prediction: an agenda for future research. In: Proceedings of the 16th IEEE International Conference on Requirements Engineering, pp. 125–134. IEEE (2008). ISBN: 0-7695-1980-6. https://doi.org/10.1109/RE.2008.48

32. Hickey, A.N.N.M., Davis, A.M.: A unified model of requirements elicitation. J. Manage. Inf. Syst. **20**, 65–84 (2014). https://doi.org/10.1080/07421222.2004.11045786

33. Hickey, A.M., Davis, A.M.: Requirements elicitation and elicitation technique selection: a model for two knowledge-intensive software development processes unsolved problem software development software solutions. In: 2003 Proceedings of the 36th Annual Hawaii International Conference on System Sciences, pp. 2005–2010. IEEE (2002). ISBN: 0-7695-1874-5

34. Hinkle, D.N.: The change of personal constructs from the viewpoint of a theory of construct implications. Ph.D. thesis. Ohio State University Columbus, pp. 1–61 (2010)

35. Jackson, M.: The world and the machine. In: 1995 17th International Conference on Software Engineering, pp. 1–10. IEEE (1995). ISBN: 0-89791-708-1. https://doi.org/10.1145/225014.225041

36. Jones, C.: Applied Software Measurement-Assuring Productivity and Quality. McGraw-Hill Inc., New York (1991). ISBN: 0-07-032813-7

37. Kalloniatis, C., Kavakli, E., Gritzalis, S.: Addressing privacy requirements in system design: the PriS method. Requir. Eng. **13**(3), 241–255 (2008). ISSN: 0947-3602. https://doi.org/10.1007/s00766-008-0067-3

38. Kang, W., Liang, Y.: A security ontology with MDA for software development. In: Proceedings of the 2013 International Conference on Cyber-enabled Distributed Computing and Knowledge Discovery, CyberC 2013, pp. 67–74. IEEE (2013). ISBN: 9780768551067. https://doi.org/10.1109/CyberC.2013.20

39. Karlsson, J., Wohlin, C., Regnell, B.: An evaluation of methods for prioritizing software requirements. Inf. Softw. Technol. **39**(14–15), 939–947 (1998). ISSN: 0950-5849. https://doi.org/10.1016/S0950-5849(97)00053-0. http://linkinghub.elsevier.com/retrieve/pii/S0950584997000530

40. Kotonya, G., Sommerville, I., Kotonya, G.: Requirements Engineering: Processes and Techniques, 1st edn. Wiley, Hoboken (1998). ISBN: 0-471-97208-8, 978-0-471-97208-2

41. Labda, W., Mehandjiev, N., Sampaio, P.: Modeling of privacy-aware business processes in BPMN to protect personal data. In: Proceedings of the 29th Annual ACM Symposium on Applied Computing, pp. 1399–1405. ACM (2014)

42. Lauesen, S.: Software Requirements: Styles and Techniques. Pearson Education, London (2002)

43. Layne, K., Lee, J.: Developing fully functional E-government: a four stage model. Gov. Inf. Q. **18**(2), 122–136 (2001)

44. Leffingwell, D., Widrig, D.: Managing Software Requirements: A Unified Approach. Addison-Wesley, Boston (2000)

45. Lim, S.L., Finkelstein, A.: StakeRare: using social networks and collaborative filtering for large-scale requirements elicitation. IEEE Trans. Softw. Eng. **38**(3), 707–735 (2012)
46. Lim, S.L., Quercia, D., Finkelstein, A.: StakeNet: using social networks to analyse the stakeholders of large-scale software projects. In: Proceedings of the 32nd ACM/IEEE International Conference on Software Engineering, vol. 1, pp. 295–304. ACM (2010)
47. Liu, L., Yu, E., Mylopoulos, J.: Security and privacy requirements analysis within a social setting. In: 11th International Conference on Requirements Engineering, pp. 151–161. IEEE (2003)
48. Loucopoulos, P., Karakostas, V.: System Requirements Engineering. McGraw-Hill Inc., New York (1995)
49. Martinez-Balleste, A., Perez-Martinez, P.A., Solanas, A.: The pursuit of citizens' privacy: a privacy-aware smart city is possible. IEEE Commun. Mag. **51**(6), 136–141 (2013)
50. Mayer, N.: Model-based management of information system security risk. Ph.D. thesis. University of Namur (2009)
51. Mead, N.: Requirements Prioritization Introduction. Software Engineering Institute Web Publication, Carnegie Mellon University, Pittsburgh, USA (2006)
52. Mouratidis, H., Giorgini, P.: Secure Tropos: a security-oriented extension of the Tropos methodology. J. Softw. Eng. Knowl. Eng. **17**(2), 285–309 (2007)
53. Mylopoulos, J., Chung, L., Nixon, B.: Representing and using nonfunctional requirements: a process-oriented approach. IEEE Trans. Softw. Eng. **18**, 483–497 (1992)
54. Nuseibeh, B., Easterbrook, S.: Requirements engineering: a roadmap. In: Proceedings of the Conference on the Future of Software Engineering, pp. 35–46. ACM (2000)
55. Paja, E., Dalpiaz, F., Giorgini, P.: Modelling and reasoning about security requirements in socio-technical systems. Data Knowl. Eng. **98**, 123–143 (2015)
56. Patsakis, C., et al.: Interoperable privacy-aware e-participation within smart cities. Computer **48**(1), 52–58 (2015)
57. Pohl, K.: Requirements Engineering: An Overview. RWTH, Fachgruppe Informatik (1996)
58. Radics, P.J., Gracanin, D., Kafura, D.: Preprocess before you build: introducing a framework for privacy requirements engineering. In: 2013 International Conference on Social Computing (SocialCom), pp. 564–569. IEEE (2013)
59. Regnell, B., et al.: An industrial case study on distributed prioritisation in market-driven requirements engineering for packaged software. Requir. Eng. **6**(1), 51–62 (2001)
60. Principles Report: PReparing Industry to by supporting its Application in REsearch. Technical report, pp. 1–60 (2014)
61. Ribeiro, C., et al.: Gamifying requirement elicitation: practical implications and outcomes in improving stakeholders collaboration. Entertain. Comput. **5**(4), 335–345 (2014)
62. Robertson, S., Robertson, J.: Mastering the Requirements Process: Getting Requirements Right. Addison-Wesley, Boston (2012)
63. Ruhe, G., Eberlein, A., Pfahl, D.: Trade-off analysis for requirements selection. Int. J. Softw. Eng. Knowl. Eng. **13**(04), 345–366 (2003)
64. Runeson, P., Höst, M.: Guidelines for conducting and reporting case study research in software engineering. Empir. Softw. Eng. **14**(2), 131–164 (2009)

65. Sabo, J. et al.: Privacy Management Reference Model and Methodology. OASIS PMRM TC Standards Track Committee Specification (2013)
66. Salnitri, M., et al.: STS-Tool 3.0: maintaining security in socio-technical systems. In: CAiSE Forum, pp. 205–212 (2015)
67. Singhal, A., Wijesekera, D.: Ontologies for modeling enterprise level security metrics. In: Proceedings of the 6th Annual Workshop on Cyber Security and Information Intelligence Research, p. 58. ACM (2010)
68. Solove, D.J.: A taxonomy of privacy. Univ. Pa. Law Rev. **154**(3), 477 (2006). ISSN: 0041-9907. https://doi.org/10.2307/40041279. arXiv arXiv:1011.1669v3. http://www.jstor.org/stable/10.2307/40041279?origin=crossref
69. Solove, D.J.: Conceptualizing privacy. Calif. Law Rev. **90**, 1087–1155 (2002)
70. Sommerville, I.: Software Engineering, 8th edn. Pearson Education Ltd., London (2007)
71. Sommerville, I., Sawyer, P.: Requirements Engineering: A Good Practice Guide. Wiley, Hoboken (1997)
72. Spiekermann, S., Cranor, L.F.: Engineering privacy. IEEE Trans. Softw. Eng. **35**(1), 67–82 (2009)
73. British Standard BS7799-1: Information security management Part 1: Code of practice for information security management (1999)
74. Bahill, A.T., Henderson, S.J.: Requirements development, verification, and validation exhibited in famous failures. Syst. Eng. **8**(1), 1–14 (2005)
75. Trochim, W., Donnelly, J.P.: The Research Methods Knowledge Base. Cengage Learning, Boston (2006). ISBN: 9781592602919
76. Tsoumas, B., Gritzalis, D.: Towards an ontology-based security management. In: 20th International Conference on Advanced Information Networking and Applications (AINA), vol. 1, pp. 985–992. IEEE (2006)
77. Van Lamsweerde, A.: Elaborating security requirements by construction of intentional anti-models. In: Proceedings of the 26th International Conference on Software Engineering, pp. 148–157. IEEE Computer Society (2004)
78. Wang, G., Valerdi, R., Fortune, J.: Reuse in systems engineering. IEEE Syst. J. **4**(3), 376–384 (2010)
79. Wohlin, C., et al.: Experimentation in Software Engineering. Springer, Heidelberg (2012). https://doi.org/10.1007/978-3-642-29044-2
80. Wuyts, K., et al.: Linking privacy solutions to developer goals. In: 2009 International Conference on Availability, Reliability and Security, ARES 2009, pp. 847–852. IEEE (2009)
81. Yu, E., Cysneiros, L.: Designing for privacy and other competing requirements. In: 2nd Symposium on Requirements Engineering for Information Security, SREIS 2002, Raleigh, North Carolina, pp. 15–16. Citeseer (2002)
82. Zannone, N.: A requirements engineering methodology for trust, security, and privacy. Ph.D. thesis. University of Trento (2006)
83. Zowghi, D., Coulin, C.: Requirements elicitation: a survey of techniques, approaches, and tools. In: Aurum, A., Wohlin, C. (eds.) Engineering and Managing Software Requirements, pp. 19–46. Springer, Heidelberg (2005). https://doi.org/10.1007/3-540-28244-0_2

The Architecture of VisiOn Privacy Platform

Amir Shayan Ahmadian[1]([✉]), Sven Peldszus[1], Jan Jürjens[1], Mattia Salnitri[2],
Paolo Giorgini[3], Haralambos Mouratidis[4], and Jose Fran. Ruiz[5]

[1] University of Koblenz-Landau, Koblenz, Germany
{ahmadian,speldszus,juerjens}@uni-koblenz.de
[2] Politecnico di Milano, Milan, Italy
mattia.salnitri@polimi.it
[3] University of Trento, Trento, Italy
paolo.giorgini@unitn.it
[4] University of Brighton, Brighton, UK
H.Mouratidis@brighton.ac.uk
[5] ATOS, Madrid, Spain
jose.ruizr@atos.net

1 VisiOn Privacy Components

The VisiOn Privacy Platform consists of a set of components and tools, which
will work and collaborate in a single platform. The overview of the VisiOn architecture is provided in Fig. 1.

1.1 Privacy Assessment Component

The two main groups of users of the VisiOn Privacy Platform are employees of public administrations (Public Administration (PA) users) and citizens.
Both groups of users have different use cases of the VisiOn Privacy Platform. The Privacy Assessment Component (PAC) addresses use cases of both
groups of users. PA users want to create questionnaires and citizens want to fill
questionnaires.

Therefore, the inputs of the component are questions that are bundled into
questionnaires. The outputs of the component are filled questionnaires, i.e., the
questions and corresponding answers. Questions can be enriched with metadata
that enables other components of the VisiOn Privacy Platform to relate the
questions and corresponding answers to data items, systems and groups of persons involved in information processing tasks. For example, if a service offered
by a PA system requires a citizen to agree on the processing of his/her personal
data, a question may read "Do you allow the PA system to store your personal
data?". The question itself is hard to interpret by software, so additional information like "dataitem=personal data; operation=store" can be attached to the
question to enable other components of the VisiOn Privacy Platform to automatically and precisely interpret citizen's privacy requirement. It is envisaged to

M. Salnitri et al. (Eds.): Visual Privacy Management, LNCS 12030, pp. 54–76, 2020.
https://doi.org/10.1007/978-3-030-59944-7_3

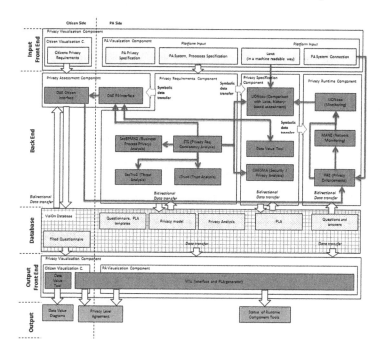

Fig. 1. The vision privacy platform architecture. (Color figure online)

have one questionnaire per PA (to support all services provided by this PA) and that a citizen will have to fill one questionnaire per PA. A citizen can update his or her privacy requirements by resubmitting a filled questionnaire where the answers reflect the updated privacy requirements. Furthermore, it is considered that the VisiOn Privacy Platform (VPP) derives certain parts of the questionnaire by using analysis results of the other components.

To explain the context of the PAC we refer to the VisiOn Privacy Platform Architecture (Fig. 1). One can see that the Dynamic Audit Engine (DAE) was planned to be the only tool of the component. The inputs of the component are the Citizens Privacy Requirements (yellow box) that have to be recorded by the PAC. Data is exchanged with the Central Privacy Database. Questionnaires filled by citizens are called Citizen Questionnaire in the figure. These filled questionnaires are used by other components as illustrated by the dashed arrow "symbolic data transfer".

The components of the VPP are grouped into a web framework and a desktop framework. The PAC is part of the web framework.

The goal of the component is the elicitation of citizens' privacy requirements. To do that, privacy requirements are formulated as questions and bundled into questionnaires by the PA. Questions are enriched with metadata that support the automatic processing of questions and their answers. Citizens are asked to answer these questionnaires in order to state their privacy requirements. The answers are exported along the questions and their metadata to the VisiOn DataBase (VDB) in two different formats. One format contains questions, answers and metadata in a machine readable document, the other format is a typeset textual representation of the filled questionnaire excluding the metadata and intended to be displayed in the Privacy Level Agreement (PLA) document.

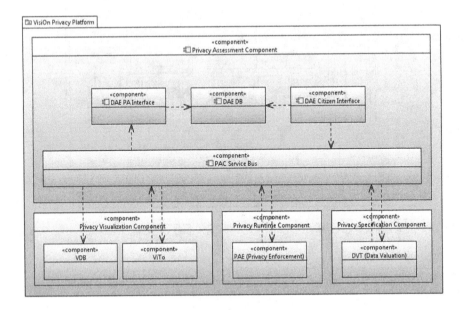

Fig. 2. The structure of PAC.

The constituent parts of the PAC are illustrated in Fig. 2. The component consists of two web based applications provided by DAE (DAE PA interface and DAE citizen interface) and the PAC Service Bus. The two web applications of DAE require another component for internal storage, the DAE DB (e.g. a MySQL database). The PAC Service Bus is responsible for the communication with other tools and components of the VisiOn Privacy Platform and contains a message bus enabling asynchronous message passing. Only those parts of the Privacy Visualization Component, Privacy Runtime Component and Privacy

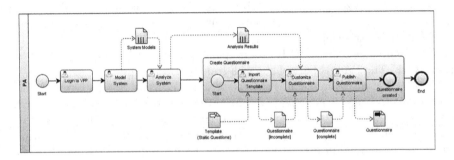

Fig. 3. The process of creating a questionnaire.

Specification Component are illustrated in Fig. 2 that directly communicate (using the VDB) with the PAC are shown.

During PA user interaction, the PA manually creates a questionnaire based on the privacy analysis results provided by the Privacy Requirements Component using the web based interface provided by the PAC, more specifically by using the DAE PA Interface. The process diagram in Fig. 3 illustrates the process of the PA with focus on the creation of a questionnaire. The sequence diagram in Fig. 4 shows the communication between PA, components of the VPP and their subcomponents during the creation of a questionnaire, while details of the actual creation of a questionnaire are abstracted.

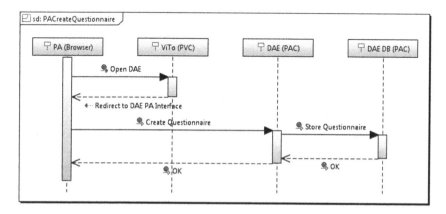

Fig. 4. User interaction of Public Administration with Privacy Assessment Component.

The citizen user interaction includes the steps of a citizen to state his or her privacy requirements by filling a questionnaire. The process of filling a question-naire is illustrated in Fig. 5. To update the privacy requirements, a citizen has to refill the questionnaire; the process is the same as for the initial filling of a questionnaire. The sequence diagram in Fig. 6 shows the communication between citizen, components of the VPP and their subcomponents, while details of how a citizen fills a questionnaire are abstracted.

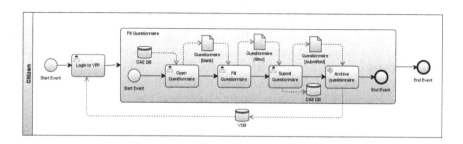

Fig. 5. The process of filling a questionnaire.

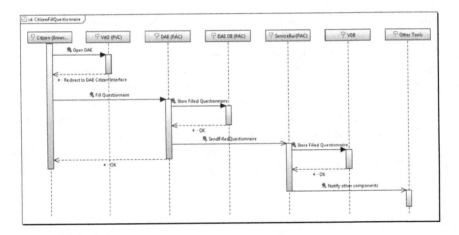

Fig. 6. User interaction of citizens with Privacy Assessment Component.

1.2 Privacy Requirement Component

Privacy Requirements Component (PRC) is responsible for the modelling and consistency analysis of citizens' privacy requirements that will be retrieved by the functionality of the PAC and for the modelling of business processes, related to Public Administrations, and verification of their compliance against organizational privacy requirements. Moreover, threat and trust analysis is conducted to the PA privacy needs and requirements.

After the Privacy Requirements analysis, the PA can use those results in order to design, or redesign (either the system is a new one or already exists, respectively) their system. Thereafter, through Privacy Specification Component (PSC), the PA can develop the UMLsec diagrams, can check the compliance of the requirements with the legal regulations and finally, can assess the value of citizens' personal data.

With the results of the different analyses, the PA can use the PAC to define the questionnaire and provide it to the citizens. A citizen fills in the questionnaire in the PAC and their answers are used by the VisiOn Privacy Platform to create the Privacy Level Agreement (PLA). The PLA is sent to the Privacy Run-Time Component (PRTC), which creates a privacy policy. The privacy policy is used to observe, verify and enforce the privacy needs of the citizen against the PA system. The status and the results of the PRTC can be seen in the PA interface of the Privacy Visualization Component (PVC). Additionally, from the PAC the results are given to the Citizen interface of the PVC.

Through the PVC, PA has an overview of the available analysis activities of the PRC and can launch the corresponding tools (see Fig. 7).

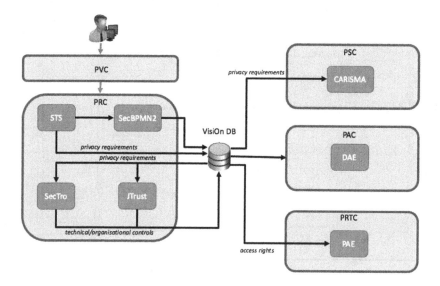

Fig. 7. Interaction of PRC tools with the VPP elements.

At first, PA uses the STS-tool to perform a privacy analysis of their system. STS-tool is able to graphically represent the purpose for which an entity has access to citizen's data. PA will use the STS-tool to graphically model the source entity and destination entity in a transmission of citizen's information. PA will also use the STS-tool to create a graphical model that visualizes privacy requirements and social and organizational aspects of the system.

PA is able to check whether its existing business processes are compliant with procedural privacy policies by using the Secure Business Process Modelling Notation 2.0 (SecBPMN2) tool. After the completion of this analysis, the produced models are stored to VisiOn Database.

Then, PA carries out, using the SecTro tool, a privacy threat analysis and identifies vulnerabilities and appropriate privacy related organizational actions and technical controls to satisfy privacy requirements and mitigate threats.

PA also identifies and justifies privacy related trust relationships, using the JTrust tool. In particular, through JTrust, PA can perform a trust/distrust analysis in order to build confidence that authorized users will not misuse their granted authorizations. JTrust tool will also support the PA in modelling trust relationships between entities and reasoning about the behaviour of those entities. Alternative solutions, such as control measures, could be identified in case that entities are not trusted.

Both SecTro and JTrust tools will use as basis STS models in order to proceed with their analysis. The produced models will be stored in the VisiOn Database. This information will be relevant to PA and the services it is offering.

Figure 8 depicts the sequence of interactions between PA and the PRC tools.

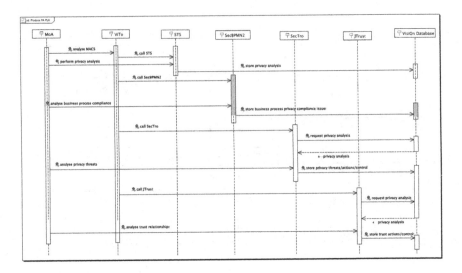

Fig. 8. PRC sequence diagram.

1.3 Privacy Specification Component

The VisiOn project aims to provide a platform to improve transparency and accountability of PA authorities. To this end, the VisiOn Privacy Platform provides citizens with the means to create and monitor a personal PLA and enables them to visualize their privacy preferences, relevant threats and trust issues. As mentioned before, the VisiOn platform consists of five core components. The PSC is responsible for specifying the PLA and indicating the citizen's data value.

The PSC is used to specify the PLA, i.e. populates the PLA with security and privacy reports, shows the compliance level with European Union (EU) privacy laws and increases awareness on data valuation. The PSC is composed of three tools, each is responsible for one of the component's functionalities.

The CompliAnce, Risk, and Security Model Analyzer (CARiSMA) tool performs security and privacy checks on PA systems by developing Unified Modelling Language (UML) models that at the end will be used to check whether these models satisfy the privacy requirements. Through CARiSMA, the PA user is able to perform information flow analysis that is able to identify potential security/privacy breaches and also to support the design of the system of the PA for assuring that citizen's information is transferred through secure channels/means. The generated security and privacy report as well as the identified risk level of citizens' critical information are transferred as part of the information included in the Privacy Level Agreement.

Moreover, PSC includes the LIONoso tool which is responsible for checking the compliance of the PA system with EU privacy laws and to estimate a score for the citizen using history-based assessment of citizen requirements and monitoring results from PRTC. The PA can use LIONoso to check the compliance of the PLA with the relevant laws and legislation. In case the PSC identifies non-compliance with law, the PA has to go back and reanalyze and redesign aspects of the system, taking into account this new information.

Last but not least, the Data Value Tool (DVT) is a tool of the component to assess the value of citizen's data. The DVT is an awareness tool that through information gathered from citizens (questionnaire), compares different perceptions on personal data valuation (e.g. data footprint, economic value, data conflicts, etc.) assisting them in the understanding of the risks and the importance when sharing data.

The tools are combined together as the Privacy Specification Component of the VisiOn platform. All the information used by the PSC is fed by the Privacy Assessment Component and in turn PSC provides input to both Privacy Requirement and Runtime Components. End-users visualization information related with the PSC (as for example the outcome of the DVT) is passed on to the Privacy Visualization Component.

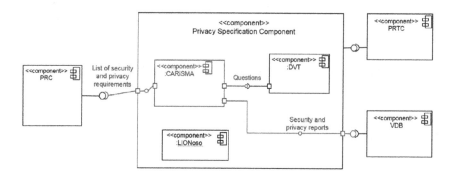

Fig. 9. Privacy Specification Component.

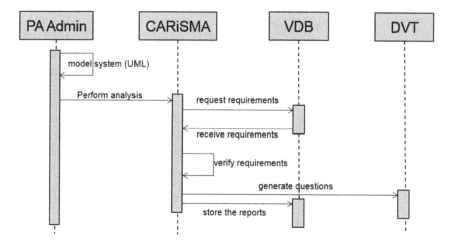

Fig. 10. Communications between PSC and the data base (VDB).

In Fig. 9 the structure of the PSC component and its interactions with the other components are demonstrated, in this figure the focus is on the process of security analysis.

Furthermore the interactions of the PSC with other tools and components are presented in Fig. 10.

1.4   Privacy Runtime Component

The Privacy Run-Time Component (PRTC) is a component that will be active during runtime. It provides different functionalities: monitoring of events in the component, monitoring data exchanged between the different pilot users provided by the Media Network Aware Element (MANE) tool and enforcing the PLA by using privacy policies provided by the Privacy Agreement Enforcer (PAE) tool.

As we have explained in the previous sections, the PRTC is in charge of real-time functionalities in the VPP. These functionalities are provided by different tools and include the generation and management of privacy policies, the enforcement of the generated privacy policies, and the process of monitoring data packet transmissions and the generation of usage and access logs. These functionalities are, in fact, the final step of the VPP, and they run continuously within the system of a PA.

As we can see in the diagram of the architecture of the VPP, the PRTC exchanges information with the other components by means of the PLA Database. These interactions are done by only two tools in the PRTC: PAE and LIONoso. The PAE reads the VDB and extracts information of the questionnaires done by the citizens in the PAC. Using this information, the PAE creates the privacy policies and stores them in a local database. Using them, the PAE can control the accesses to the data. The LIONoso tool, on the other hand, exchanges information of the logs of the PAE and the MANE in order to show it to the citizens or public administration.

Regarding internal interaction in the PRTC, the tools work very closely. The PAE, by controlling accesses to the data generates logs about the rules and accesses that are used by both the LIONoso and the MANE. On the one hand, the MANE uses the information of the rules for controlling data packet exchange in the PA system and also generates logs about them. On the other hand, the LIONoso uses the logs generated both by the PAE and the MANE for statistics and information for the citizens and the PA. It requests the information to both tools depending on the time constraint defined for it (the polling can be hourly, daily, etc.). In the following sections we describe more in depth each tool of the PRTC, its functionality and interaction with the other tools.

The Privacy Run-time Component works at run-time, its main goals are:

- Monitoring the events and traffic: this will provide citizens and PAs a way of controlling who is requesting the data, also helping ensure that the privacy preferences set by the citizen are being fulfilled.

- Evaluating the requests concerning citizens' privacy preferences: the main goal is to ensure that the privacy preferences of the citizens control the accesses to data. Therefore, these preferences are considered by the VPP to evaluate received data.

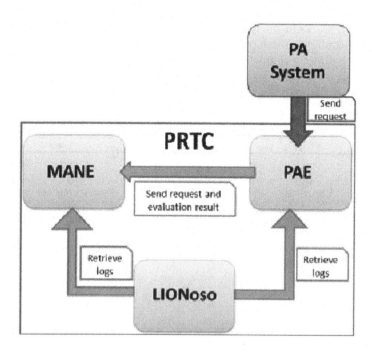

Fig. 11. PRTC abstract diagram and interactions.

The PRTC is formed by three different tools, which are: PAE, MANE and LIONoso. Each described in more detail in their own section (Integrated Tools).

Figure 11 shows the interaction between the tools in the component and how the component reacts to an external request from the PA system. The figure helps explaining the functionalities of the component, which focus on fulfilling the goals, which are the following:

- PAE: enforcement of the privacy preferences. Privacy policies are generated for each citizen according to the privacy preferences provided and all requests to access the protected data are evaluated against the policies. This fulfills the goal of "Evaluation of requests based on citizens' privacy preferences", since these preferences are first transformed into privacy policies and then any received request is evaluated against them.
- MANE: Monitoring and filtering the network traffic. Acts as an extra layer of data protection by applying access rules according to the data received from PAE. This fulfills the goal of "Monitoring of events and traffic", specifically monitoring the network traffic through the platform.

- LIONoso: Monitoring of events by reading and parsing logs of PAE and MANE tools. It extracts features from logs to use as the training data for the history-based assessment in the PSC and to display them as notifications in the PVC. This fulfills the goal of "Monitoring of events and traffic", since it will be reading this information from the logs of MANE and PAE.

The PRTC works in the background as part of the VisiOn Privacy Platform. The PA can configure some options of the component, but besides that, it will work by being directly contacted by the PA system to evaluate requests to access citizens' data.

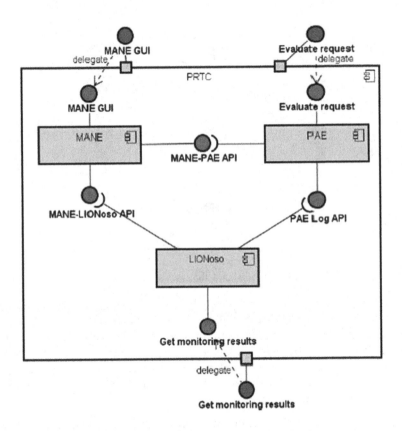

Fig. 12. The component diagram of PRTC.

Figure 12 displays the component diagram, showing the interfaces exposed by each tool to interact among them and also the interfaces that the component will expose either to other components or to the PA system. As can be seen, there are three interfaces that the component exposes to interact with other components:

- MANE Graphical User Interface (GUI): is the Graphical User Interface that MANE offers. It can be used by the PA administrator to configure MANE or to check information about MANE.
- Evaluate Request: this interface is meant to be used by the PA system to send requests to access citizen's data. The requests are sent to the PAE tool to be evaluated against the privacy policies which were created according to the privacy preferences provided by the citizen.
- Get monitoring results: this interface is provided by LIONoso and it provides all the information it has retrieved and parsed from both MANE and PAE logs. This information describes the requests that both tools have received as well as the responses to these requests.

As the figure shows, there are also some internal interfaces which were developed in order to integrate the different tools inside the component:

- MANE-PAE API: this interface is provided by MANE and used by PAE to send the requests and the results of evaluating these requests. This information is then used by MANE to generate network rules.
- MANE-LIONoso API: this interface is provided by MANE and used by LIONoso to retrieve the logs that the MANE tool has generated from monitoring the network access.
- PAE log API: this interface is provided by PAE as an API so that LIONoso can obtain the logs where the information about the requests and the results of their evaluation are stored.

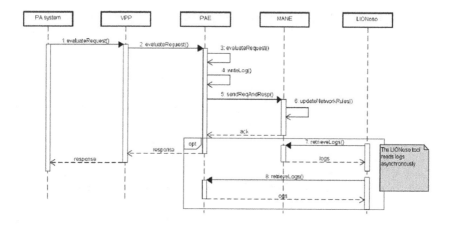

Fig. 13. Request evaluation sequence diagram.

Figure 13 demonstrates a sequence diagram to specify how the interfaces displayed in Fig. 12 are used. There are eight interactions in this sequence diagram that can be explained individually:

1. The process starts when the PA sends a request to be evaluated to the VPP.
2. The VPP, where the PRTC is integrated, redirects the request to the PAE.
3. The PAE takes the request and evaluates it against the correspondent privacy policies.
4. After the evaluation, the PAE tool writes a log including the request and the response (result of the evaluation). This log is made available through the log manager API so that LIONoso can retrieve it.
5. The PAE tool sends the request and the response to the MANE tool through the interface exposed by MANE.
6. The MANE tool receives the request and the response in XACML format, updating its network rules accordingly to the information received.
7. Here starts a process which is asynchronous. This process is started by LIONoso and on this step it uses the interface exposed by MANE to retrieve its logs.
8. To finish the process, the LIONoso tool retrieves the logs of the PAE tool through the log manager API.

As explained in the sequence diagram, there are two different processes: one synchronous and one asynchronous. The synchronous process goes from the first step to the sixth. Part of the process is also the response. This response includes the result of the evaluation of the request against the privacy policies protecting the requested resource. The response is therefore generated by the PAE tool and is sent to the PA system.

1.5 Privacy Visualization Component

The VPP has two conceptual subcomponents, which provides user interfaces to citizens and PA administrators. These subcomponents allow the user to select the functionalities of the platform and to enter the data. These are (Fig. 1):

- The Citizen Visualisation Component (CVC): Guides the citizens to submit or change their privacy requirements using the questionnaire provided by the DAE tool of PAC. Next, it allows the citizen to view the Privacy Level Agreement (PLA) created by the privacy requirements provided by the citizen and the PA. Finally, it displays data value diagrams generated by the Data Value Tool (DVT) of the Privacy Specification Component (PSC).
- The PA Visualisation Component: Allows PA administrators to monitor the status of the runtime component tools by displaying notifications of Privacy Run-Time Component (PRTC) and to define the questionnaire for the citizen using the DAE tool. This component also includes STS, SecBPMN2, JTrust, SecTro, CARiSMA to manually pre-analyze the system which are part of PRC and Privacy Specification Component (PSC). These tools have their own interface and they are installed and launched independently.

Furthermore, citizens and PA administrators use Visualization Tool (ViTo) and Data Value Tool, which are directly a part of this component to perform additional visualization functionalities. These tools are implemented as web based tools in order to provide to the citizens and PA administrators online access using a wide range of devices. Therefore, it is not required for the citizens and PA administrators to install third party software and a recent browser will be adequate in order to access the VPP interface.

The Privacy Visualisation Component provides both an input front-end and output front-end for citizens and PA administrators.

- Citizens are able to:
  - submit their privacy preferences using the DAE tool of the PAC,
  - display and download their PLA using ViTo of the PVC,
  - display their data value diagrams using DVT of the PVC.
- PA administrators are able to:
  - create questionnaires using the DAE tool in PAC, pre-analyse system using STS, SecBPMN2, JTrust, SecTro of the PRC, LIONoso and CARiSMA of the PCS,
  - monitor, access and configure using PAE and MANE of the PRTC,
  - display PLAs, data value diagrams and runtime notifications using ViTo and DVT of the PVC.

STS, SecBPMN2, JTrust, SecTro, and CARiSMA are desktop-based tools and have their own user interface. They work independently and store their results directly to the VDB. DAE, MANE, PAE, and LIONoso provide web-based access for the PA administrators integrated as a web-based framework. PVC also provides web-based interfaces, both for input and output to the citizens and PA administrators, to interact with the platform.

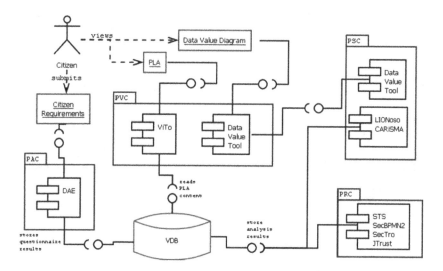

Fig. 14. Citizen's interaction with PVC.

Concerning Fig. 14, the CVC allows citizens to submit their requirements using DAE tool of PAC, to display PLA created using their requirements and PA system analysis results in ViTo and to display their data value diagrams created by DVT in PSC. As presented in Fig. 14, PVC interacts with PSC directly and interacts with PAC and PRC via VDB. Citizens describe their privacy requirements using DAE tool in PAC. Their requirements are stored in VDB and later displayed them as a part of their PLA. DVT primarily operates in PSC and stores its results in VDB and displays data value diagrams to the citizens in PVC. PRC and PSC analysis tools store their results in VDB and PVC displays these results as a part of PLA of the citizen. PVC assists the citizen to interact with the VPP easily from one central interface.

Concerning Fig. 15, the PA Visualization Component carries out the visualization tasks of the PA administration of the platform. It directly interacts with PA administrators and allows them to perform the following tasks:

- It provides a page to list PLAs of all the citizens who submitted their privacy requirements by filling the questionnaire.
- It provides a page to list all the notifications extracted by log monitoring of the tools in the PRTC.
- It allows to create and update questionnaires via DAE in PAC.
- Tools of the PRC and the PSC are accessible independently to perform the analysis.

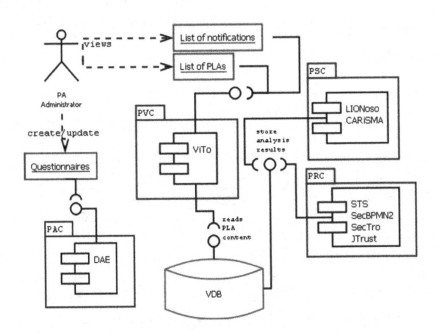

Fig. 15. PA's interaction with PVC.

2   Integrated Tools

2.1   DAE

In companies, many different questions have to be answered during the normal business or especially during audits. Mostly a single person cannot answer these upcoming questions. Therefore, Fraunhofer ISST has developed the DAE to lower the staff time and effort, which is needed to delegate questions and gathering the information. DAE tool of the Fraunhofer ISST will perform the elicitation of the user privacy needs using as basis for the information input the data provided from the public administrations.

2.2   STS-Tool and SecBPMN2

Socio Technical Security-Tool (STS-Tool) (developed by the University of Trento) [4,5] is a software for enforcing social and organizational security requirements in business processes. It permits to (i) specify social and organizational security requirements using a goal based modelling language, (ii) specify business processes with security concepts using an extension of BPMN 2.0; (iii) verify the enforcement of the security requirements in the business processes; (iv) generate security documents that contain the information specified in the models and the results of the analysis. STS-Tool already integrates SecBPMN2 as a plugin. The STS-Tool can be used to address many issues related to privacy.

Analysis of complex organizations: Many PAs are complex organizations composed by technical components and people. In such organizations the verification of the enforcement of privacy requirements is a complex and error-prone task. The STS-Tool can be used to automate this task, remarkably reducing its time of execution and eliminating the errors that a person may commit. Fast adaptation to external changes: The automated verification of privacy allows a fast adaptation of the PA organizations when security requirements change because of external factors. For example, when a law on privacy is modified, a modification of the security policies on privacy is enough to check if the PA organization is compliant or it shall be adapted. Moreover, the STS-Tool indicates where the security issues are, and therefore, it helps security analysts in identifying the problem and, therefore, in solving it.

Within the VisiOn Privacy Platform, STS-Tool can be used as part of requirements engineering, having its derived (social) security requirements translated/mapped to technical security/privacy specifications, to ease the transition from the requirements phase to the system design phase.

2.3   Sectro and JTrust

Secure Tropos (developed by the University of Brighton) [6] is a security-aware software systems development methodology, which combines requirements engineering concepts, such as actor, goal, plan together with security engineering concepts such as threat, security constraint and security mechanism, under a unified process to support the analysis and development of secure and trustworthy software systems.

The idea is, for Information Technology (IT) related users that work for public administration organizations, to use SecTro and identify privacy related threats and; vulnerabilities that exist in their systems. Moreover, the tool identifies the appropriate security and privacy mechanisms that are necessary in order to protect their systems against the identified threats. To this end, SecTro will support the PA IT employees with a library of privacy threat pat-terns and also a library of PET that mitigate privacy threat. Additionally, SecTro will feed the Privacy Visualization Component with information about privacy threats and then be presented to the citizen/patient in a user friendly and understandable way.

The JTrust tool (provided by the University of Brighton) is a graphical editor supporting the modelling of trust and control, and the automatic assessment of system's trustworthiness in the JTrust methodology. The tool supports modelling of system dependencies, resolutions, and entailments, and performs an automatic assessment of the system's trustworthiness based on the identified system dependency resolutions.

The idea is that IT related users that work for Public Administration organizations to use JTrust in order to model the privacy related trust relationships that affect the trustworthiness of their systems in terms of ensuring privacy. Then, to reason about these trust relationships in a structured way and to identify technical or organizational controls in cases where there are gaps of trust in order to ensure that data privacy is pre-served.

2.4 LIONoso

LIONoso (developed by the University of Trento) is a platform for data analytics that focuses on visualiza-tion, modelling (predictive analytics) and optimization (prescriptive analytics). In the setup phase, the user defines a workflow (by means of a visual tool) by combining various modules for data input and manipulation, model creation (factories), prediction and optimization, visualization. The workflow structure can then be hidden from the final user, who can use LIONoso as a black box that reads or receives data from a source and produces graphical and textual reports, predictions and recommendations.

Within the VisiOn Privacy Platform, LIONoso will be used to: (1) Verify the compliance of a PLA with a set of rules representing the relevant EU privacy laws, and (2) try to identify potential problems that a citizen could face during his interaction with the PA by examining past cases of citizens with similar privacy requirements. In the latter context, LIONoso will complement rule-based tools by providing an additional heuristic evaluation, which will prove useful in reducing potential grey areas and will help assess novel cases.

2.5   CompliAnce, Risk, and Security Model Analyzer (CARiSMA)

Modelling allows the design of high-quality critical systems and identification of security requirements/properties during the design time in order to provide a natural integration of security in the system. CARiSMA [1–3] provides an opportunity to perform compliance analysis, risk analysis and security analysis of software models. Generally, CARiSMA provides a platform to model system architectures using UMLsec diagrams. Moreover, it supports and implements UMLsec checks. Due to its EMF-based implementation, CARiSMA can also support domain-specific modelling languages such as BPMN. A flexible plugin architecture makes CARiSMA extensible for new languages and allows users to implement their own compliance, risk, or security checks. In the VisiOn platform, CARiSMA is used to perform a security and privacy analysis. The PA system architecture is modelled as a UML diagram, afterwards the UML diagrams are annotated with security and privacy requirements. The CARiSMA performs different security and privacy checks to verify PA systems. At the end CARiSMA generates a report, informing about the security and privacy threads and vulnerabilities.

2.6   Media Network Aware Element (MANE)

MANE (developed by NCSRD, National Centre for Scientific Research "Demokritos") is capable of applying Deep Packet Inspection (DPI) for packet filtering at both the network and the application layer. The DPI approach indicates that network flows are inspected and information is extracted from higher layers of packet data (up to the application layer). By exploiting the rich high layer information that is provided through DPI, contents' aware network node control functions can provide various options in packet flow handling, for instance, information about the enforcement of privacy policies. NCSRD's DPI software called MANE can locate, identify, classify, reroute and block packets with specific payload, something that is not possible with conventional packet filtering techniques that assess only packet headers.

MANE is extended to accept and parse VisiOn privacy policies in the format that they will be submitted. Additionally, they will have to be translated from the privacy policy format into real time network traffic rules, and be applied accordingly.

2.7   Privacy Agreement Enforcer (PAE)

The PAE (developed by ATOS) provides two main functionalities. On the one hand, it provides functionalities for managing users' privacy policies, allowing them to create, remove and modify the level of privacy protection that they want to apply to their personal information. On the other hand, it has an engine in charge of ensuring that any given request trying to access a protected resource has to comply with h the policies that have been described by the owner of that information, granting access only when these policies are satisfied. PAE will be extended in VisiOn in order to allow users who do not have knowledge about XACML to also be able to manage their XACML privacy policies. In addition, PAE will protect private data by providing accesses only to authorized users and complying with the privacy policies defined by the data owners.

2.8 Data Value Tool (DVT)

Data valuation is the process to identify which information is most important and most valuable. In others words, it is a promise of value to be delivered and a belief of the receiver that the value will indeed be delivered and experienced. Personal data valuation is a complex and difficult task and while no commonly accepted methodology exists, two main approaches can be identified:

- market valuation of the data, i.e. market cap/revenues/net income per data record, market prices for data, cost of a data breach, data prices in illegal markets are some of the proposed methods to estimate the value of personal data.
- individual perceptions of the data value, i.e. surveys and economic experiments used to estimate the individual valuation of personal data and the individual valuation of privacy.

In VisiOn project the DVT aims to capture the perspective of citizens in regards to the data they are willing to share and the importance they have about these data and compare this with both the PA's expectations and average users' perspective. To achieve its goals, the DVT uses the VisiOn questionnaire to gather input from both the PA and the citizens, calculates metrics based on the answers and visualizes the results to the users.

3 VisiOn Database

The PLA is one of the central elements of the VPP, since it will contain, for each citizen, her privacy preferences and other useful information to be used by the PA when accessing her data. For this reason, it is required to have all the PLAs centralized in a database where all the different components of the VPP can access it, either for adding new data or for managing it.

With this in mind a database was created to contain all the information required to generate a PLA for each citizen, providing an API that all tools could use to access it easily. The database will store two different types of documents: specific for the PA and specific for each citizen. The documents specific for the PA will contain information about the system that the PA uses, such as models.

The VPP consists of different tools that generate outputs with variable types. Therefore, it is important to use a storage system that can handle large files, several formats, and multi-structured data types. One typical solution is using non-relational databases to meet these requirements. Although there are many different solutions, MongoDB distinguishes between these solutions by being easy to install, having support in many different languages and frameworks, having a permissive commercial license to use, and high popularity, which makes it have a big community. It is the fourth most popular database management system in overall, and most popular for document stores according to DB-Engines Ranking.

MongoDB simplifies storage of various models created by the tools in the platform by being a document-oriented database. Document-oriented databases are general purpose, useful for a wide variety of applications due to the flexibility of the data model, the ability to query on any field and the natural mapping of the document data model to objects in modern programming languages.

MongoDB is also an agile database that uses a flexible document data model so schemas can change quickly as applications evolve. This flexibility allows us to write and read information in various formats to the database and adapt the document model to our needs easily.

For the integration process this flexibility that MongoDB provides is very useful, but at the same time the capability of storing large files is perfect for the VPP, since it will store different kinds of documents, such as models, which can get potentially very large. To be able to provide easy access for all the components of the VPP to the PLA database a REST API was created. This RESTful API provides different functions to create, read, update and delete data from the database.

Having an API instead of allowing direct access to the database is helpful for security reasons, making components database agnostic so that if any details about the database are modified the components will not require any further modification since the API will stay the same.

4   Vision Framework

When designing the VPP, we noticed we had very different tools with different objectives and that providing all of them in a single framework (e.g. same technology, usage, etc.) and, after several discussions, we decided it would be better to have different frameworks due to the nature, characteristics and goals of the different tools we have in VisiOn. This way, we have tools that were desktop base (heavy-processing) and other were web-based (accessible from any location at any time). Therefore, the web-based framework could cover all the tools for working with the generation and management of the privacy preferences, reports, data value, etc., which by being online would improve vastly the impact and usability of the platform. On the other hand, the desktop-based framework contains the tools for modelling and generation of privacy reports of the system, so they could fit better to be used in a desktop by expert users.

Together with these two frameworks we need a back-end that provided all the interfaces for communication between the component and tools and a database that was created for facilitating the exchange of data between them. This database provides an API that the tools and components use for storing and retrieving data, allowing an easier and faster communication between the two frameworks (web and desktop). The design of the two frameworks and the back-end followed the architecture defined in Fig. 1, as it clearly identified the interactions between the tools and components, and the list of the VPP requirements. That way, these two frameworks cover all the necessities of the Public Administrations and citizens in an easy and simple way. Following we describe more in-depth each of the frameworks and the back-end.

4.1 VPP Back-End

The VPP back-end provides all the internal functionality, interactions and exchange of data in the VPP, more specifically for the two frameworks developed in the project: web and desktop frameworks. Therefore, it provides a database (VisiOn database) that is used for storing and retrieving data by the tools of the VPP components. This way tools can exchange data as they need and it is also used for generating the PLAof each citizen, as it contains all this data provided by the tools. The access and interaction with the database is done by means of an API, which aims to facilitate the work with the database and also makes easier to create new functionalities for the database or modify the existing ones. This component acts as a pivotal element for interconnecting the tools, components and framework as can be seen in the Fig. 1 of the architecture of the VPP.

4.2 Web Framework

Web applications allow users to access universally from any computer with and Internet connection and a browser supporting latest web technologies without requiring any prior installation. For these reasons, tools that are part of assessment, runtime and visualization components are integrated as a web framework to allow citizens and PA administrators to access the platform easily. The web framework will be used by several users, both citizens as well as members of the PA. To control the access to the different functionalities of the platform it was deemed necessary to include an authentication and authorization mechanism.

4.3 Desktop Framework

The VisiOn Desktop Framework integrates the components and tools more heavy-processing that are used by the PAs for modelling. This framework runs in the computer of the Public Administration and allows it to design and specify privacy and security analysis of their system (either new or existing one) in order to a) obtain information about privacy issues that will be used in the creation of questions later in the VisiOn Web Framework and b) provide security and privacy reports of the system of the PAs. The VisiOn Desktop Framework is connected with the VisiOn database in order to exchange data and communicate with other tools and components of the VisiOn Web Framework.

The usual work with this framework done by the PA is as follows, although it is not mandatory to do it in this way or even go through all the tools. Each of them provides a report with specific characteristics and descriptions of the system under development or existing so it depends on the PA which tools they want to use. Through the tools that belong to the Privacy Requirements Component, the PA can use the STS tool to identify and collect privacy requirements and the SecBPMN2 tool to check the compliance of the business process with procedural privacy policies. Then, with the usage of the SecTro tool the PA can analyze privacy threats and identify system vulnerabilities. The use of Sec-Tro also allows the PA user to define appropriate privacy related organizational actions and technical controls that satisfy privacy requirements and mitigate threats. Finally, the PA can use the JTrust tool for privacy related trust relationships, mitigation actions and organizational actions.

In addition, the desktop framework will support the Public Administration (PA) in the system design. In particular, through the Privacy Specification Component, the PA can use the CARiSMA tool to perform proper privacy and security checks in order to analyze the system design and architecture. To this end the PA requires the PA's system models and the SRS file generated by the STS tool, which contains the list of security and privacy requirements. The system models are expressed as UML diagrams that the PA can annotate with relevant security and privacy requirements and perform the checks. Finally, through the LIONoso tool, the PA can check the compliance of the requirements with the legal regulations, and through Data Value Tool the PA assesses the value of given citizens' personal data (e.g. data footprint, economic value, data conflicts, etc.)

Acronyms

PA	Public Administration
EU	European Union
PLA	Privacy Level Agreement
VPP	VisiOn Privacy Platform
PET	Privacy Enhancing Technology
UML	Unified Modelling Language
GUI	Graphical User Interface
SecBPMN2	Secure Business Process Modelling Notation 2.0
PAC	Privacy Assessment Component
PRC	Privacy Requirements Component
PSC	Privacy Specification Component
PRTC	Privacy Run-Time Component
PVC	Privacy Visualization Component
VDB	VisiOn DataBase
DAE	DynamicAudit Engine
DVT	Data Value Tool
CVC	Citizen Visualisation Component
ViTo	Visualization Tool
IT	Information Technology
CARiSMA	CompliAnce, Risk, and Security Model Analyzer
PAE	Privacy Agreement Enforcer
STS-Tool	Socio Technical Security-Tool
MANE	Media Network Aware Element

References

1. Ahmadian, A.S., Strüber, D., Riediger, V., Jürjens, J.: Model-based privacy analysis in industrial ecosystems. In: Anjorin, A., Espinoza, H. (eds.) ECMFA 2017. LNCS, vol. 10376, pp. 215–231. Springer, Cham (2017). https://doi.org/10.1007/978-3-319-61482-3_13
2. Ahmadian, A.S., et al.: Model-based privacy and security analysis with CARiSMA. In: Proceedings of the 2017 11th Joint Meeting on Foundations of Software Engineering, ESEC/FSE 2017, Paderborn, Germany, 4–8 September 2017, pp. 989–993 (2017). https://doi.org/10.1145/3106237.3122823
3. Jürjens, J.: Secure systems development with UML. Springer, Heidelberg (2005). https://doi.org/10.1007/b137706. ISBN 978- 3-540-00701-2
4. Paja, E., Dalpiaz, F., Giorgini, P.: STS-tool: security requirements engineering for socio-technical systems. In: Heisel, M., Joosen, W., Lopez, J., Martinelli, F. (eds.) Engineering Secure Future Internet Services and Systems. LNCS, vol. 8431, pp. 65–96. Springer, Cham (2014). https://doi.org/10.1007/978-3-319-07452-8_3
5. Paja, E., et al.: Specifying and reasoning over socio-technical security requirements with STS-tool. In: Ng, W., Storey, V.C., Trujillo, J.C. (eds.) Conceptual Modeling, vol. 8217, pp. 504–507. Springer, Heidelberg (2013). https://doi.org/10.1007/978-3-642-41924-9_45
6. Pavlidis, M., Islam, S.: SecTro: a CASE tool for modelling security in requirements engineering using secure tropo. In: Proceedings of the Conference on Advanced Information Systems Engineering (CAiSE) Forum, pp. 89–96 (2011)

Visual Privacy Management

Sven Peldszus[1]([✉]), Amir Shayan Ahmadian[1], Mattia Salnitri[2], Jan Jürjens[1], Michalis Pavlidis[3], and Haralambos Mouratidis[3]

[1] University of Koblenz-Landau, Koblenz, Germany
{speldszus,ahmadian,juerjens}@uni-koblenz.de
[2] Politecnico di Milano, Milan, Italy
mattia.salnitri@polimi.it
[3] University of Brighton, Brighton, UK
{m.pavlidis,h.mouratidis}@brighton.ac.uk

1 Introduction

In this chapter, we focus on the privacy and the security analyses of public administration (PA) systems regarding the privacy concerns and requirements. As it has been described in the architecture of VisiOn, the VisiOn Privacy Platform is composed of two frameworks and a common back-end that provides internal functionalities, data storage, etc. A high-level demonstration of the VisiOn Privacy Platform (VPP) is provided in Fig. 1. The two main frameworks are VisiOn Desktop Framework and the VisiOn Web Framework. Each has unique goals, requirements, functionalities. The PAs use both however a citizen only interacts with the desktop framework.

The desktop framework mainly aims to perform a privacy analysis. The above mentioned analysis relies on model-based analysis methodologies. Analyzing system models allows a system designer to focus on specific aspects of the systems—such as privacy and security—and identify privacy and security threats from the early phases of the system development. Several modeling tools are integrated into the VisiOn Privacy Platform to conduct the privacy and security analysis.

The VisiOn web Framework is the main interface for citizens in order to access information about how their data is managed, and to define their privacy policies. Moreover, public administrations will be able to use web framework for generation of questions, check how the access to the data of the citizens they have is accessed and by whom,

In the following sections, we briefly introduce the two frameworks and their respective tools. According to the VisiOn Privacy Platform (VPP) architecture, the tools are integrated into different components. We support these components in this chapter by describing the tools and their integration into the VPP.

M. Salnitri et al. (Eds.): Visual Privacy Management, LNCS 12030, pp. 77–108, 2020.
https://doi.org/10.1007/978-3-030-59944-7_4

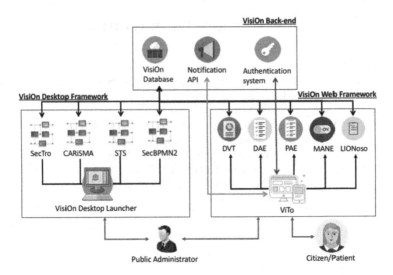

Fig. 1. A High-level demonstration of the VisiOn Privacy Platform Architecture.

2   Desktop Framework

The VisiOn Desktop Framework contains the components and modelling tools that are used by the Public Administrations (PAs) to perform security and privacy analysis of their system, allowing them to obtain more information which can be used for the creation of questions in questionnaires.

2.1   Privacy Requirement Specification

According to the principles of privacy and security by design [8], such concepts have to be considered as early as possible during the design of complex systems such as the PAs. The VisiOn Privacy Platform (VPP) supports such principles by integrating a set of software tools that allows the definition of privacy and security requirements in the early stage of the design of PA systems and during all software requirement phases, until the complete definition of requirement for PAs. In particular, VPP integrates 4 Tools: Socio Technical Security-Tool (STS-Tool) [5], Secure Business Process Modelling Notation 2.0 (SecBPMN2) [24], SecTro [16,20] and JTrust [22,23]. The rest of the section describe each tool and it's integration into the VPP.

STS-Tool

Socio-Technical security (STS) [5] is a tool that helps VPP users to define privacy and security requirement of PA systems. Such systems are called socio-technical since they include autonomous actors (both humans and technical ones) that interact in order to achieve common objectives. PA system are socio-technical since are composed by citizens and PA employees that interact with PA services.

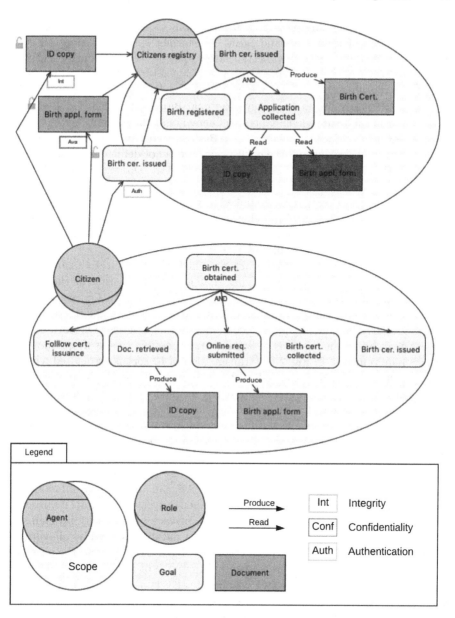

Fig. 2. Example of a STS-ml social-view (Color figure online)

Socio Technical Security - modelling language (STS-ml), the language used by STS, has been already described in a previous chapter. Therefore, we will introduce only the concepts used for the integration with other frameworks, for a comprehensive description of STS-ml please refer to [5].

Figure 2 shows an example a STS-ml diagram. Using STS-ml is possible to define two types of actors: role and agent. The former specifies a group of components, for example citizens, while the latter specifies a single, well identified, component, for example the citizen registry. Each actor has a scope, in which are defined the objectives of the actors, that are called goals. For example, the agent Citizen Registry wants to achieve the goal Birth Cert. issued. Goals can be decomposed in sub-goals, which express refinements of the decomposed goal. For example, Birth Cert. issued is decomposed in Birth registered and Application collected. Please notice that, in STS-ml, the concept of time is not defined, therefore, there is no indication in which goal has to be achieved before. Documents can be placed inside the scope of an actor and represent physical supports that contain information used by actors. Documents are linked to goals with a relation that indicates how such documents are used to achieve the goal. Such relation can be Read, if the document will be read to achieve the goal, or Produce if the document will be created when the goal is achieved.

Goal can be delegated, between actors, which means that the source actor transfers the responsibility of achieving that goal to the target of the delegation. For example, the goal Birth cert issued is delegated from Citizens to Citizen Registry. As a result, Citizen Registry will inherit the goal (highlighted in dark green). Similarly documents can be transmitted between actors. On both delegations of goals and transmissions of document, is possible to specify privacy and security requirements. In Fig. 2 the transmission of ID copy is associated with an integrity requirements, which specifies that the communication channel used for the transmission must guarantee the integrity of the document transmitted. Similarly, the transmission of Birth appl. form is associated with Availability security requirements, which specify that the communication channel should be always available to send the document. The delegation in the example is linked to an authentication privacy requirements, which specifies that the actors who delegates and the one that receives the delegation have to be authenticated.

STS-Tool [25], the software that supports STS, can analyze STS-ml models in order to highlight syntax errors and privacy and security errors that, if unsolved, might lead to the design of a PA system with privacy and security problems.

STS-Tool is integrated into the VPP using a database shared by all software tool used in VPP (called VisiOn DataBase or VDB). STS-Tool use the database as a workspace in order to increase the productivity of PA users and help user to share their STS-ml models and collaborate. Every time a PA user modifies a STS-ml model, the file where the model is stored is locked, preventing the modification from other users. When the user closes the diagram, the file becomes modifiable to all other PA users. Yet PA users can open the STS-ml model in a read-only mode. This mechanism prevents conflicts yet al.lowing many users to access the model.

When a PA user decides that the model is complete he can export it in the database, at this point the model becomes available to other tools that will used it as a starting point for their analyses.

SecBPMN2

Business processes are central in most of PA organizations since they describe the order of activities that have to be executed by PA employees and citizens to reach certain objectives. SecBPMN2 [24] is a framework which allows to defined business processes with a focus on privacy and security concerns. SecBPMN2 is composed of two languages: SecBPMN-ml, for the definition of business processes with security annotations, and SecBPMN2- Query language (SecBPMN2-Q), an extension of SecBPMN2- modelling language (SecBPMN2-ml) for the definition of security constraints on business processes, called privacy and security policies (security policies for short).

Figure 3 shows an example of a SecBPMN2-ml diagram. SecBPMN2-ml is based on **BPMN! (BPMN!)** 2.0 [18]: two pools represent a Citizen and the Citizens registry. Inside each pools there is a process which starts with a Start event and ends with one or more End events. The main element of **BPMN!** is the Task, which is an atomic unit and represents a set of actions, while the main relation is the Flow relation which represents the order of execution of activities. Gateways represent choices in the business process execution. In Fig. 3 the XOR gateway Correct will direct the execution on the upper path if the answer is yes otherwise it will direct the execution to the lower path. The two pools are connected with a Message flow which specifies that the Citizen sends the ID copy to the Citizens registry.

SecBPMN2-ml extends **BPMN!** 2.0 with security annotations which represent security mechanisms to be enforced when the business process is implemented and then executed. Figure 3 shows two security annotations: (i) availability, that it is linked to the message flow and specifies that the communication channel should be always ready to send and receive messages; (ii) Non-Repudiation, which specifies that the execution of the activity linked, i.e., Create copy of ID, should be legally provable.

SecBPMN2-ml specifies business processes with security annotations. Its natural extension, i.e., SecBPMN2-ml, is a modeling language used to specify privacy and security policies, in terms of procedural constraints, on such business processes. Figure 4 shows two examples of security policies specified with SecBPMN-Q. Security policy 1 specifies that the communication channel used between Citizen and citizen registry to transmit ID copy should be available. this policy is verified in the business process specified in Fig. 3, since the security annotation in the business process matches the one in the security policy. More refined parameters, such as the value of the availability can be specified and are used in the verification. For more information on the verification, please refer to [24].

Security policy 2 introduces a new relation specific for SecBPMN2-Q, called walk. A walk relation connects two tasks and specifies that, in the business process analyses, the first task should be connected to the second one with an arbitrary sequence of executable elements. In particular, security policy 2 specifies that Create copy ID should be connected with Send ID. Security policy 2 is verified in the business process specified in Fig. 3, since Create copy ID is connected with Send ID through the task Find address.

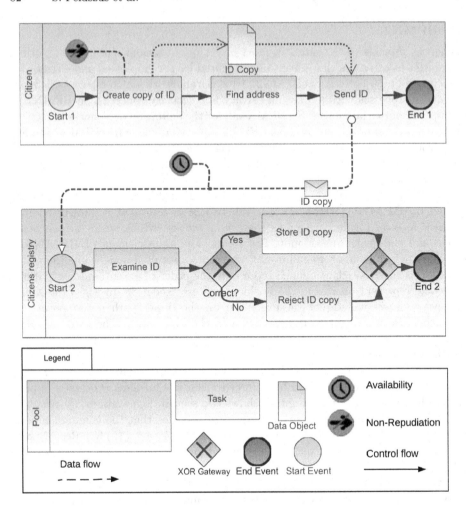

Fig. 3. Example of a SecBPMN2-ml business process

We integrated SecBPMN2 in VisiOn Privacy Platform (VPP) connecting it with STS-Tool. The definition of business process specifies that a business process is executed to achieve one or more objectives, we therefore connected the goals (i.e., objectives) that can be specified in STS-ml with the objective in the definition of business processes, where one STS-ml goal is achieved by the execution of one or more SecBPMN2 processes. We also defined a mapping relation between security requirements, defined using STS-ml, with security policies defined using SecBPMN2-Q. We automated most of the transformation in order to ease the life of VisiOn users: a skeleton of business processes can be generated in an automated fashion and the generation of security policy is completely automated.

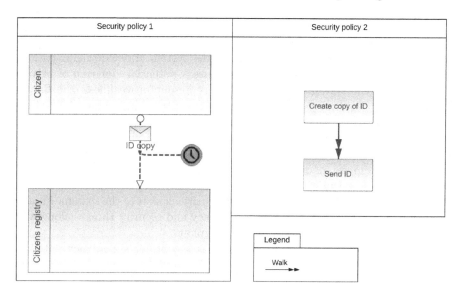

Fig. 4. Example of two SecBPMN2-Q security policies

Similarly to STS-Tool, SecBPMN2 saves all partial models directly on the databases, therefore PA user can easily share their models and work from different computers. SecBPMN2 is integrated with other tools using the VisiOn database: when a user considers the SecBPMN2 model complete, the tool publish the model in the database and, therefore, it will available to other VisiOn frameworks.

SecTro

The SecTro tool [20] is a modelling tool for the Secure Tropos methodology [16]. Similarly with STS-ml, SecTro's modelling language is a goal based language, that allows a system designer to specify mechanisms that are required in order to satisfy privacy and security requirements. Also, SecTro enables modelling of privacy related threats and vulnerabilities of a system under development. This allows the system designer to reason about these privacy threats and vulnerabilities and identify privacy and security mechanisms that can be used to protect against the identified privacy threats. To further support a system designer a privacy patterns library is accompanying the tools that includes privacy pattern with their respective Privacy Enhancing Technologys (PETs).

SecTro's main concepts are the Privacy and Security Constraints which represent the privacy and security requirements respectively. In the context of software engineering a constraint is usually defined as a restriction that can influence the analysis and design of an information system under development by restricting some alternative design solutions. Other important concepts are the Privacy and Security Mechanisms. These represent technical or organization mechanisms that support the satisfaction of privacy and security constraints. In the context of privacy threat modelling the main concept is the Threat which represents a circumstance that has the potential to cause loss or a problem that can put in danger the privacy and security features of the system under development. An Attack Method is an action that aims to cause a potential violation of privacy and security in the system. A Vulnerability represents a weakness or a flaw in terms of security and privacy that exists in the system, and vulnerabilities can be exploited by attack methods.

The above mentioned concepts belong to different views in SecTro. Each view denotes a specific phase of activity in the modelling process. The main goals of the system are modelled in the Organizational View of the system under development. The Security Requirements View of the system provides a more detailed representation of the privacy and security aspects of the system. Finally, the Security Attacks View describes the privacy and security threats along with the vulnerabilities of the system that they exploit.

The Privacy Patterns Library of SecTro is a contains six privacy patterns: i) Anonymity and Unlinkability; ii) Anonymity and Pseudonimity; iii) Undetectability; iv) Unlinkability and Undetectability; v) Unlinkability; vi) Unobservability (Anonymity and Undetectability). Each privacy pattern contained in the library includes alternative privacy mechanisms that can be implemented in order to satisfy the relevant privacy requirement. It is up to the software engineer to select the ones that are more suitable for the system under development and also by considering the advantages and disadvantages of the mechanisms, such as their usability and monetary cost. The Undetectability privacy pattern is depicted in Fig. 5. The Figure shows the Anonymity privacy constraint and the four privacy mechanisms that can satisfy this constraint along with their submechanisms.

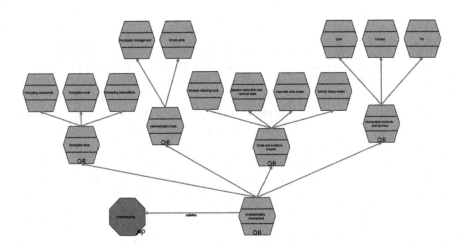

Fig. 5. Undetectability pattern

In the context of the VisiOn platform, SecTro is using the shared database. The privacy and security requirements, along with the organization models, are automatically retrieved from the from the models in the shared database that were created with the **STS-tool! (STS-tool!)**. The import of the STS-ml model to SecTro is accomplished according to the transformation rules depicted in Table 1.

Table 1. Transformation rules

STS-ml	SecTro & JTrust
Agent/Role	Actor
Goal	Goal
Document	Resource
Delegation	Secure dependency
ANDOR	ANDOR
Privacy requirement	Privacy constraint
Security requirement	Security constraint

Then, the system designer can extend the models by adding additional privacy and security requirements and identify and model suitable privacy and security mechanisms that satisfy the privacy requirements utilizing the Privacy Pattern Library. Furthermore, the software engineer can model privacy threats and reason about how well the system under development would be able to protect against such threats. Supplementary privacy mechanisms can be identified to mitigate potential privacy threats.

SecTro Illustration

Going back to the running example of the citizen of Athens, the Municipality of Athens (MoA) system designers use the SecTro tool in order to extend the STS model with privacy threats along with the appropriate privacy and security measures to protect against these threats and satisfy the identified privacy and security requirements.

An outcome of the privacy analysis of the Athens PA system is the identification of a number of privacy and security requirements. One privacy requirement identified with STS-ml is to prevent unauthorized detection with regards to the birth certificate, or in other words the privacy requirement is undetectability with regards to the birth certificate. Undetectability refers to the prevention of a third party from distinguish whether the citizen who requests the birth certificate is a user of the system or not. A security requirement identify with STS-ml is that at no point an authorized third party should have access to the Birth Certificate itself. To satisfy the undetectability privacy requirement the PA system engineer can utilize the privacy pattern library of the SecTro and select a suitable privacy mechanism. In this case, a set of administrative tools was selected, such as smart cards and permission management, along with the anonymizer mechanism TOR, to satisfy the privacy requirement for undetectability as depicted in Fig. 6. This analysis enables the justification of why the specific privacy mechanisms need to be placed and added to Municipality of Athens system. In the Security Requirements view the PA system engineer can also identify potential threats that can endanger the security of the system. In this case Tampering has been identified as one potential threat against the confidentiality of the Citizen's Birth Certificate.

The Tampering Threat is further elaborated in the Security Attacks View as depicted in Fig. 7. The Birth Certificate is considered as data at rest when it is stored in the database and can potentially be seen or modified by unauthorized entities. To protect against these types of attacks a Host Intrusion Detection System (IDS) and encryption have been identified as security mechanisms that have to be implemented.

The models created by the SecTro tool are stored in the shared database of the VisiOn platform and are used by the rest of the tools of the platform.

JTrust

The JTrust tool [22,23] is a software tool that supports a methodology for modelling and reasoning about trust relationships within an information system and for assessing the trustworthiness of that system. In the context of the VisiOn platform, JTrust's main functionality is to enable a PA software engineer to model and reason about trust relationships that can impact the privacy of the information of the citizens. In the past it was easier for a system be developed trustworthy, as it was very simple, isolated, and only depending on itself.

Modern information systems though include not only technical components but also human components that exist in the environment of the technical components. There is a distinction between the technical component, which is one or more machines that behave in a way to satisfy the requirements with the help of the software, and the environment, which is the part of the world with which the machine will interact and in which the effects of the machine will be observed. Modern information systems therefore comprise socio-technical infrastructures that include large numbers of actors, including humans. Due to the need for constant interaction and communication with other systems and humans, which do not belong to their infrastructure, technical components need to interact with systems and humans that they might not have interacted before. In fact, they might depend on other systems and/or humans to accomplish tasks and operations that directly affect their operation in terms of ensuring security and privacy. Consider for example the scenario where an information system depends on another system for information that is crucial for completing some of its security operations. In such scenario, trust, to both humans and other systems, is an important issue for modern information systems as they depend on entities (humans and systems), over which they do not have direct control, for resources to achieve their security and privacy requirements. It is therefore important, in

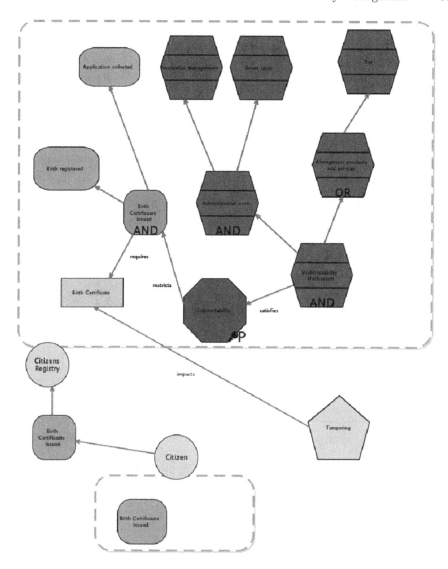

Fig. 6. Security Requirements View

order to understand the risks involved in such dependencies, to understand the various trust relationships that an information system might be part of. Trust is therefore is not only an enabler of security [21] but also an enabler of privacy. Modelling of trust relationships with the JTrust tool surfaces the gaps in the chain of trust relationships and the assumptions made about these. Such assumptions are made by developers and/or stakeholders related to the various trust relationships that exist within an information systems and are underlying the analysis of the system and can undermine its trustworthiness in terms of

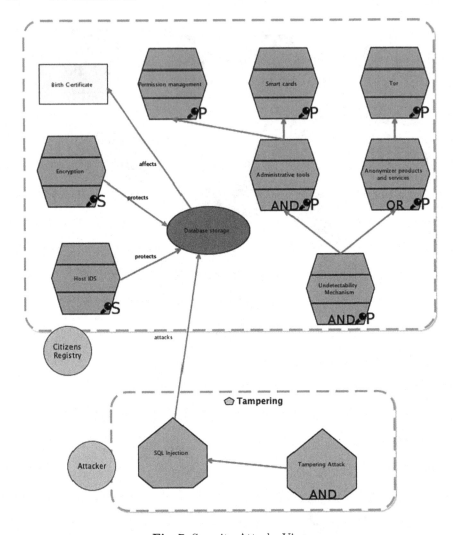

Fig. 7. Security Attacks View

ensuring privacy and security. These gaps are explicitly identified by the tool in a systematic and structured way, offering the capability to specify control mechanisms that need to be in place in order to protect data privacy because of lack of trust.

The JTrust modelling language extends the SecTro modelling language by adding concepts related to trust and control. The main concept is the concept of Resolution. A Resolution is the means to offset the potential vulnerability that a dependency on a human or system component introduces. In order to find resolutions the system designer needs to ask the question of why does he feel confident that the entity assigned with a privacy or security task will complete successfully the task hence fulfill the dependency. The resolutions essentially reveal the assumptions that must be valid for the system to be built on strong foundations. There are two types of resolution, trust and control resolutions. Trust Resolution indicates that the system designer trusts that the entity assigned with a task will fulfill the dependency by achieving the task once the information system-to-be is put in operation. Trust resolutions can be of four different types:

- Experiential Trust is trust that originates from previous direct experience with the trustee. The parties have verifiable information by first hand inter-actional or transactional experience with each other.
- Reported Trust is trust that originates from a third party (the reporter) who reports that the trustee is trustworthy. This is valuable when the trustor does not have first-hand information of the trustee.
- Normative Trust is trust that originates from the system environment norms. Trustees are motivated to behave in a specific way by their desire to act in accordance with internalised norms.
- External Trust is trust that originates from sources outside of the system environment. Such sources can be laws and external policies.

The other type of resolution is Control Resolution. Control is a key source of confidence and is the power that one actor has over another actor to influence their behaviour. In essence, when a system designer uses a control resolution as a resolution of a dependency this means that they are confident that the dependee will fulfill the dependency by achieving the task once the system is put in operation, because either the depender or another actor is controlling the dependee and forcing them to do so Control requires knowledge and influence from the depender's side. Knowledge specifies the ability of an actor to gather information about another actor's behaviour in order to decide whether to execute an action that will directly influence her behaviour. In addition, control specifies the action that is required for the dependee to behave in an expected way. In other words, control is in place in order to punish the depender in case of deceitful behaviour. We define two concepts that represent the above notions, observation and deterrence: Observation is the continuous examination of whether that dependee actor is behaving as expected and she is fulfilling a dependency. It is required as part of an effective control mechanism in order to alert that a dependency is not being fulfilled and possibly to trigger further actions. Deterrence is the prevention of a dependee's goal in case she fails to fulfill a dependency, so that it can influence her behaviour. Only through observation a control mechanism cannot be effective. It requires also an action that can be taken against a dependee who fails to achieve a goal of a dependency. This action should prevent the dependee from accomplishing one of his own goals, so eventually it will influence her behaviour. The more important is the dependency for the depender the more important the goal that is prevented should be. Deterrence acts both as a threat and as a punishment for the dependee. The last concept is the concept of entailment, which is a condition of trust that is required to be valid for having confidence in the dependency from which it is originally generated. Entailments are created because of the resolutions that have been defined by the system designer and are essentially the trust assumptions that are underlying the development of the system.

Because the JTrust modelling language extends the SecTro modelling language, the JTrust tool was integrated within the SecTro tool and is represented as another view, named Trust View. Similar to STS-ml and SecTro, the JTrust is using the shared VisiOn database. The organizational setting along with the privacy and security requirements are imported from the STS-ml tool using the same transformational rules presented in Table 1. When the system designer completed the trust models developed with JTrust, these are saved in the shared database and the information that is contained is used by tools of later stages of the VisiOn platform.

JTrust Illustration

In the running example of the citizen of Athens, the PA system designer once they have used the SecTro tool to identify privacy and security mechanisms in order to satisfy the privacy and security requirements and mitigate threats, they can use JTrust in order to reason about the trust relationships within the information system. This step will help them identify and assumptions about trust relationships that are not valid and can constitute vulnerabilities of the system in terms of ensuring data privacy and security.

To this end, the PA system designers construct, with the use of JTrust tool, a trust model, as shown in Fig. 8. The dependencies between the actors are automatically imported from the STS tool. The PA system designer adds the two new dependencies on the actors that are assigned with satisfying the privacy and security requirements. In our case, we consider the privacy requirement for undetectability of the birth certificate, and the security requirement that only authorized entities should have access to the birth certificated. The entity assigned with satisfying these two requirements is the Citizens Registry, and therefore these are two trust relationships with the Citizens Registry that have to be examined whether they are valid or not. If the assumptions made about these trust relationships are wrong then this may have an impact on the privacy and security of birth certificate. The dependency on the Citizens Registry to prevent unauthorized entities from accessing the Birth Certificate is resolved with an Experiential Trust Resolution and the trust relationship is justified. The PA system designer has direct experience with the Citizens Registry and there is evidence that it will provide the Birth Certificate only to authorized entities. However, in the case of the dependency on the Citizens Registry to ensure undetectability of the Birth Certificate there is no trust and therefore the dependency is resolved with a Control Resolution. As a result the dependency has to be resolved with a Control Resolution. The Control Resolution identified is that the Municipality of Athens is controlling the Citizens Registry and it will enforce them to ensure undetectability. Therefore, this creates a new dependency on Municipality of Athens to control the Citizens Registry. The newly introduced dependency, and therefore trust relationship, is justified with normative trust, which is trust that is based on the norm of the system's environment. The three entailments identified in the model represent the underlying trust assumptions. These were investigated during the domain analysis and found to be valid. If there were cases where there was lack of trust then control mechanisms would have to be added in order to enforce the fulfillment of goals such as visiting times to be kept confidential.

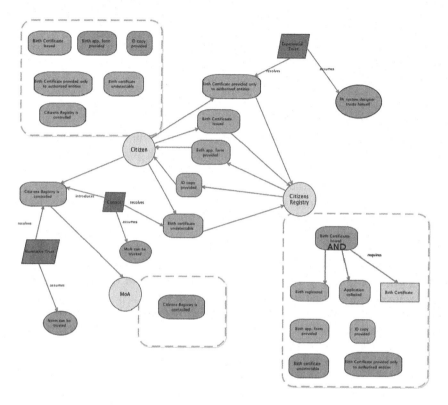

Fig. 8. JTrust model of the Birth Certificate example

2.2   Privacy Analysis Based on System Models

In the previous section, we described how privacy and security requirements are modeled—using STS-Tool and SecBPMN2. In this section we explain the privacy and security analysis of a system model. A system, is modeled using Unified Modelling Language (UML) diagrams [19] Using UML models developers can express the structure and behavior of a system – e.g. which subsystems are communication with each other over which physical or logical connection and which part relies on security properties of which other part.

UMLsec [11] provides a possibility to express privacy and security proper-ties in UML diagrams. These properties may be analyzed for completeness and consistency by set of security and privacy checks, revealing possible privacy and security threats. The checks are implemented in the $CARiSMA$[1] tool. Technically, the UML profile mechanism is used to define a profile, which provides stereotypes for annotating specified types of UML elements. Stereotypes may have tagged values.

The UML system models and the models generated by STS-Tool express a system from different perspectives. Furthermore, the annotation of the UML diagrams conforms to the security and privacy requirements, specified by the models generated by the STS-Tool. We first introduce the UML system models, afterwards, we explain the annotation of the UML diagrams with the UMLsec profile. Afterwards, we present the privacy and security checks, which conduct the security and privacy analysis.

UML Model of the System

The structure and the behavior of the system for issuing birth certificates in the municipality of Athens has been modeled with UML. In this chapter, we consider the class, deployment, and state machine diagrams.

The class diagram contains three classes representing the institutions and persons involved in a request of a birth certificate. These are two public administrations involved in the issuing of a birth certificate, represented by the classes *AthensMunicipality* and *CitizensRegistry*, and a class for the citizens requesting a birth certificate (*Citizen*). Furthermore, one class represents the form and data of a request (*BirthCertificateRequest*) and one class the birth certificate itself (*BirthCertificate*). A central datastore is represented by the class *MACS*.

Citizens can request a birth certificate by creating an instance of *BirthCertificateRequest* and passing it to *CitizensRegistry* by calling the operation *requestBirthCertificate(BirthCertificateRequest):BirthCertificate*, in case the citizen is a Greek citizen. The *CitizensRegistry* forwards the request to the *AthensMunicipality* and handles the billing of the request for which (e.g.) a discount can be granted. If the request is valid, the *AthensMunicipality* issues the birth certificate in the *MACS* by calling *issueBirthCertificate():BirthCertificate* and returns it to the *CitizenRegistery*.

During this procedure, some data is stored temporarily and some even permanently. For example, the *BirtCertificateRequest* is stored by the *CitizensRegistry* until the *BirthCertificate* has been returned to the *Citizen* and the *MACS* permanently stores all issued birth certificates.

From a security point of view, it has to be ensured that an unauthorized third party has no access to the sensitive data such as the unique identification number of citizens (*AMKA*) or the *BirthCertificate* itself.

---

[1] http://carisma.umlsec.de.

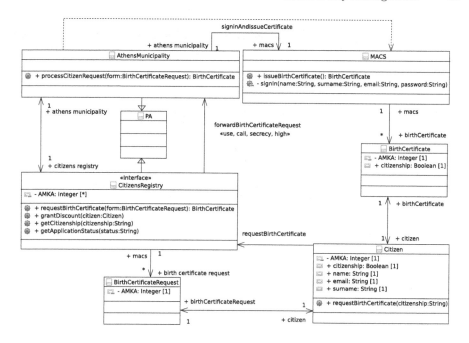

Fig. 9. UML class diagram of the system

UMLsec Secure Dependencies

When a citizen –e.g. George– is requesting a birth certificate he relies on the citizens registry to obey his security requirements for sensitive data. For example, citizens should expect that all their data, provided to the citizen registry by requesting a birth certificate, are protected from unauthorized access and manipulation of a third party (enduring *secrecy* and *integrity*). Those security requirements on dependencies are expressed in the UMLsec secure dependencies check. In this check, the defined security requirements for data and processes have to be obeyed by both sides of dependencies. Therefore, developers specify their required and provided security properties on the according classes in a UML class diagram representing the system. If inconsistencies between the annotations of e.g. different development teams occur those are detected by CARiSMA and can be considered while development.

In Fig. 10, an excerpt of a class diagram illustrating the structure of the system is demonstrated. The citizen itself has only contact to the citizen registry. The process of the request is shown in the class diagram as *«use»*-dependency *requestBirthCertificate* between the classes *Citizen* and *CitizenRegistry*. More precisely, the operation is called by a citizen.

The security requirements of the citizen are stated in the *«critical»* annotation in the class *Citizen* by listing the signatures, for which specific security requirements are requested or provided. In the class *Citizen*, accordingly to the discussed security requirements, secrecy and integrity are stated for the signature

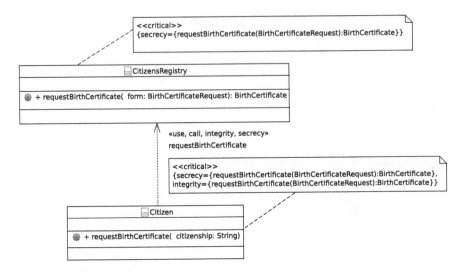

Fig. 10. Excerpt from the class diagram in Fig. 9 with security annotations for secure dependencies

requestBirthCertificate(BirthCertificateRequest):BirthCertificate. Since the class *Citizen* does not define such a signature, it requests those properties from other classes implementing this signature. Furthermore, all relevant dependencies have to be annotated with *«call»* or *«send»*. The fact that the call itself obeys the secrecy and integrity security requirements, is stated with the *«integrity»* and *«secrecy»* stereotype on the dependency. Such a dependency is annotated with *«call»* or *«send»* and refers to a class with a signature for which a security property is given either in a *«critical»* stereotype at a class either on the left hand side or the right hand side of the dependency is secure if the same security properties are given for this signature at the other side of the dependency.

Considering the example in Fig. 10, secrecy is defined on both sides of the dependency called *requestBirthCertificate* for the signature *requestBirthCertificate(BirthCertificateRequest):BirthCertificate*, however, integrity is missing in the class *CitizensRegistry*. Therefore, the secure dependency check is violated in this case. The citizens registry does not support all security requirements specified on the classes used by it.

Mappings Between SecBPMN2 Elements and UML Elements

Defining all security requirements is a time taking and challenging task. Moreover, all security requirements have to be supported in all development steps of software projects. Many of the relevant security requirements have already been considered at requirements engineering and also have to be supported in the system models. CARiSMA may conduct a pre-analysis on the output of the STS-Tool together with the UML system models to assist system designers by the annotation of the UML system diagrams with UMLsec annotations [2].

CARiSMA provides a report, suggesting a mapping between the elements of the STS's output and the UML diagrams. This report enables one to annotate the UML diagrams with the appropriate stereotypes.

```
1  | role = Citizen |
2  | role = Citizens Registry |
3  | security requirement: authenticationDelegation |
4  | security requirement type: delegatee |
5  | CARiSMA check = RABAC |
6  | UML Diagram = Class Diagram & State Machine |
7  | Document : BirthCertificate is mapped to Class:
       BirthCertificate. |
8  | Role: Citizen is mapped to Class: Citizen. |
9  | Role: Citizens Registry is mapped to Class:
       CitizensRegistry. |
```

Listing 1. One entry form the mapping from STS to UMLsec

For example, according to the STS model shown in Fig. 2 users with the role *Citizen* need authentication (*Auth*) if they want to read their birth certificate produced by the citizens registry (*CitizenRegistry*). The suggestions of *CARiSMA* for realizing this security requirement on the UML models are given in Listing 1. In lines 1 and 2 are the relevant roles listed and in lines 3 and 4 the requirement for authentication of the accessing citizen by the citizens registry. For both roles, corresponding classes (*Citizen* and *CitizensRegistery*) are defined in the UML class diagram in Fig. 9 as well as the class *BirthCertificate* representing the according document form the STS model, which is also stated by CARiSMA in the lines 7 to 9. A suggestion is to model this security requirement with a CARiSMA check called *RABAC*, which will be introduced in detail in the following section.

Role-Attribute-Based Access Control (RABAC)

Access control is one of the most important security mechanisms for ensuring security and privacy of information. Using access control we can control who has access to sensitive data and can read or change the data. One mechanism for access control is to give roles to users which are combined with specific rights.

In our system for example the citizens registry could have many employees of which only some are allowed to issue birth certificates. Therefore, those employees have a role –e.g. called *citizensRegistry*– which the other employees don't have. The rights of the role *citizensRegistry* for example might be *read*, *modify* and *produce*. Specific action like e.g. the issuing of a birth certificate by calling the operation *issueBirthCertificate():BirthCertificate* of the class *MACS* in Fig. 9 can be combined with necessary rights. In this case a user would need the right *produce* to issue a new birth certificate.

Comparable to the secure dependencies check the RABAC profile of CARiSMA allows developers to annotate UML models with this information.

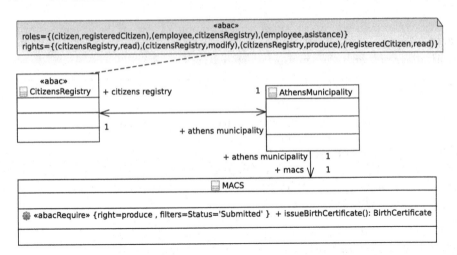

Fig. 11. Excerpt from the class diagram in Fig. 9 with security annotations for RABAC

In Fig. 11, the excerpt from the class diagram in Fig. 9 is shown, which is relevant for RABAC. Available roles and rights are specified in the tagged values of the *«abac»* stereotype, which e.g. can be attached to classes on which the access control should take place. Considering this, the class *CitizensRegistry* at which the employees processing birth certificate requests, is employed. The roles are given as a list of tuples in the format *(subject, role)*. In the example, the subjects *employee* and *citizen* and the roles *registeredCitizen*, *citizensRegistery* and *assistance* are defined in the tagged value *roles*. While the citizens can only have the role *registeredCitizen*, the employees can have the roles *citizensRegistery* and *assistance*. The rights are defined in the tagged value *rights* as tuples in the format *(role, right)*. While the role *citizensRegistry* has the discussed rights, the role *assistance* has no rights and *registeredCitizen* only the *read right*. Which rights are required to perform a specific action like issuing a new birth certificate by calling the operation *issueBirthCertificate():BirthCertificate* of the class *MACS* is given in the tagged value *right* of the *«abacRequire»* stereotype of the according class member. Considering these annotations, a classical role based access control may be performed to verify which subjects can access which properties and operations in the class diagram. In the example shown in Fig. 11, only the subject *citizensRegistry* can call the operation *issueBirthCertificate():BirthCertificate*.

The role-attribute-based access control extend this concept with attributes containing additional conditions which have to be fulfilled. One attribute is the tagged value *filters* of the *«abacRequire»* stereotype. For instance, the filters may state specific variables have specified values. In the example, the annotated operation can only be called if the status attribute has the value *Submitted*. For more details please have look at the work of Ahmadian et al. [1].

CARiSMA's RABAC analysis now allows to generate access policies from this annotations, to check who can access which content under which circumstances and retrieve the actions that a subject can perform, when the system is in a specific status. For example in Fig. 11 the subject *employee* only has the right to issue a birth certificate if it has the role *citizensRegistry* and the value of *Status* is *Submitted*.

Performing CARiSMA Checks

Our tool CARiSMA has been implemented as a plug-in for the Eclipse Integrated Development Environment (IDE).[2] In Fig. 12 is a screenshot of an Eclipse with CARiSMA and the Papyrus UML editor shown. On the left hand side of the figure you can see the Papyrus editor showing the view on the UML model which is shown in Fig. 10. If we want to analyze this UML model we have to define an analysis configuration. In CARiSMA, security and privacy analyses can be configured in *.adf files. In the screenshot you can see on the right hand side such an analysis configuration called *model_ analysis.adf*. In this analysis are the secure links and the RABAC analysis for getting possible actions for a specific system configuration selected. Which specific configuration should be analyzed is given as a XML file on which we will have a closer look later.

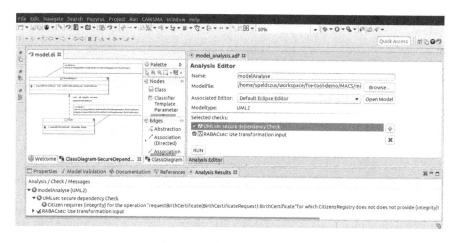

Fig. 12. Screenshot of analysis configuration and check results in CARiSMA

As during the analysis of the STS output relevant UMLsec checks and annotations are suggested to developers we can also use this information for automatically initialize a CARiSMA analysis configuration file. This analysis configuration file contains analyses for all UMLsec checks suggested to developers and can be manually extended. Furthermore, necessary information like the UML model which should be analyzed are automatically set.

When we execute such an analysis configuration by clicking the *RUN* button in the center of the figure, the selected checks and analyses are executed and

---

[2] http://eclipse.org/.

the *Analysis Results* view on the bottom of the figure is populated with status messages. In the screenshot we can see that the security violation discussed earlier has been detected by CARiSMA and the precise location of the violation is given.

```
1   <?xml version="1.0" encoding="UTF-8" standalone="yes"
        ?>
2   <rabac>
3       <sessions>
4           <entry>
5               <key>employee</key>
6               <value>
7                   <set>citizensRegistry</set>
8               </value>
9           </entry>
10      </sessions>
11      <attributes>
12          <name>Status</name>
13          <type>User</type>
14          <values>
15              <entry>
16                  <key>employee</key>
17                  <value>Submitted</value>
18              </entry>
19          </values>
20      </attributes>
21  </rabac>
```

Listing 2. RABAC configuration (rabac.xml)

The configuration which has been analyzed by the RABAC analysis is the one given in Listing 2. From lines 3 to 10 the session which should be considered is configured and in lines 11 to 20 the values of the attributes. In this case we want to know which actions a subject with the key *employee* and with the set of roles [*citizensRegistry*] can perform, when the attribute with the name *Status* has the value *Submitted*. This configuration represents exactly the same scenario as considered earlier in this work.

In the output of CARiSMA we can see that the RABAC analysis has been executed successfully. The detailed results of the analysis are visible when we export an analysis report.

For the RABAC analysis performed in this example the output is given in Listing 3. As expected the considered employee can call the operation *issueBirthCertificate():BirthCertificate*. Additionally this user has the right to call the operation *grantDiscount(Citizen)* which has been defined in the class *CitizensRegistry* of Fig. 9 and has also been annotated with an «*abacRequire*» stereotype in the complete model.

```
1  Running check : RABACsec: Use transformation input
2  Configuration : rabac.xml
3  --------------------------------------------------------
4  User employee has access to the following protected
       items:
5    issueBirthCertificate
6    grantDiscount
```

Listing 3. Report for the RABAC analysis

3   Web Framework

The VisiOn Web Framework is composed by four components: PAC, PSC, PRTC and PVC. The VisiOn Web Framework focuses in allowing the definition and •description of the privacy preferences for the citizens, and logging and informing citizens about the accesses to their data.

PA administrators use the web framework to define privacy preferences of their systems, to specify policies, to check accesses to the data they store and the internal value of data of the citizens (using self-estimated values). Citizens use the web framework mainly to define their preferences for the privacy management of their data (e.g. do you allow the data you provide to be used by a third party? do you allow your clinical data to be shared with another doctor for a second opinion?). Together with this, they may check the accesses to their data (who accessed, for what reason, when, etc.). Moreover, they may check the internal value of the data they provided according to the estimation of the public administrations and, finally, consult everything in a user-friendly way thanks to the Privacy Level Agreement (PLA). The PLA contains all its information regarding privacy preferences and acts as a *contract* between the citizen and the public administrations.

3.1   Privacy Assessment Component (PAC)

The PAC addresses use cases of PAs and the citizens. A PA want to create questionnaires and citizens want to fill questionnaires.

Dynamic Audit Engine (DAE)

The DAE is a general purpose survey engine addressed to end users with limited technical knowledge. It is a modified version of the Software JDeSurvey [10] that has been published under GNU Affero General Public License version 3 (AGPLv3) [27] by JD Software Inc. During the VisiOn project, several improvements and enhancements were implemented. Some of them are generic ones, while others are VisiOn specific and probably will not be used in other contexts than the VisiOn Privacy Platform.

One of the necessary and important modifications was the added possibility to attach specific metadata to questions. That way, questions can be formulated in natural language and described in a machine-readable way. This modification includes the adjustment of Dynamic Audit Engine (DAE)'s data model in order to hold and linger metadata that has been attached either to questions or to options of questions in case of multiple-choice or single-choice questions, where the set of answers is predefined. Metadata are basically a key/value pair of strings. The set of strings used for keys is not predefined or restricted, therefore this functionality is not VisiOn specific.

In order to support single-sign-on mechanisms the application had to be decoupled from its own user management and authentication system. The formerly tight coupling of the application with its user management and authentication system had to be dissolved. This demanded modifications across many parts of DAE affecting several levels of the application architecture.

The previously limited granularity of ways to adjust the application's functionality, depending on assigned roles and authorizations, was dramatically · increased. Where the application formerly assumed three fixed roles, the application can now handle arbitrary many roles that are mapped to application specific authorizations. By that, functionalities can be provided or forbidden for certain users depending on their roles.

The integration with the VisiOn Web Framework, was improved with regards to the design of user interfaces. The user interfaces were fundamentally redesigned using the Twitter Bootstrap Framework[3] since across the technical partners of VisiOn it was agreed on using that reliable, mature, hence simple to use layout framework to harmonize the look and feel.

One of the fundamental enhancements of the DAE was the design and construction of an additional service, the communication service bus. The Communication Service Bus (CSB) is a supporting, internal component offering no direct functionality to users. It eases the integration of DAE with other services. The DAE was modified to send filled questionnaires to the CSB, which sends two representations of a filled questionnaire to the VisiOn DataBase (VDB), one JSON encoded representation and one HTML representation for the direct embedding in the PLA.

To support the pilot partners in creating questionnaires, different questionnaire templates have been created. The templates include examples of questions that are enriched with metadata in the way they are expected by other tools of the VPP. The CSB periodically reads these questionnaire templates from VDB and sends them to DAE, where the PA users can import the questionnaire templates to create new questionnaires.

Along with these example questionnaire templates, one question template is generated based on information contained in the VisiOn database as a result of an analysis performed in the VisiOn Desktop Framework. The CSB periodically reads the STS model from the VDB, parses the model, extracts modelled authorizations and rephrases as questions those authorizations of the

---

[3] http://getbootstrap.com/.

STS model, that have to be given by the data subject (citizen). The questions are enriched with metadata that are understood by Privacy Agreement Enforcer (PAE). The enriched questions are bundled into a questionnaire template that is stored to the VDB. This automatically created questionnaire template is imported by the previously described mechanism into DAE. That way the PA can model in a graphical way questions that are used to gather their consents to certain data processing intents. Based on the authorizations modeled in STS, and the citizens' consents elicited by DAE, the PAE creates data access policies. This is achieved by reading the JSON representation of the generated questionnaires filled by citizens and exported to VDB.

The Data Value Tool (DVT) of the Privacy Specification Component requires some information from the PA. This information is elicited by an additional questionnaire that has to be filled by the PA. This special case is treated differently compared with the questionnaires filled by citizens. When the PA fills a questionnaire, the results have to be stored at a dedicated location in the VDB. That way the DVT knows that the answers are the answers representing the PA's assessment of certain data value related aspects.

Similarly to the previous, the PA has the option to fill a questionnaire containing questions that are used to assess a PA's compliance with data protection laws. Once, this questionnaire is filled by the PA, the JSON representation is again stored to a dedicated location in VDB. LIONoso picks up the answers and performs an assessment of compliance with data protection laws based on the answers given by the PA.

3.2   Privacy Run-Time Component

The Privacy Run-Time Component (PRTC) provides several functionalities such as: event monitoring, the exchanged data monitoring (provided by Media Network Aware Element (MANE)), and enforcing the privacy level agreements (PLAs) using privacy policies (provided by the PAE tool).

LIONoso

LIONoso is a Machine Learning framework developed by the Machine Learning and Intelligent Optimization research group at the University of Trento. It provides an integrated framework for reading, processing and visualizing data; processing capabilities lie within the area of supervised and unsupervised machine learning. The LIONoso core library, written in C++ for efficiency purposes, has been compiled for all major operating systems and CPUs. With the exception of a small number of bug fixes, the core library has not been modified within the course of the project; however, it has been complemented with various Java modules for integration within the VisiOn Privacy Platform. In particular, a LIONoso Java/Tomcat service has been implemented to expose the necessary functions by a user-consumable web interface and for interoperation with the other web framework components. A description of the custom-written components follows.

The Notification Module periodically extracts information from the logs generated by the other PRC tools, namely PAE and MANE, and stores the results in a database. This process has two objectives:

- Organize the data so that it can be efficiently displayed in tabular form by the Privacy Visualization Component,
- Periodically compute the request rejection rate (number of PA information access requests rejected by PAE divided the total number of requests) for every citizen, which is used by the History-based assessment module.

The module has been modified to accommodate for the presence of optional or alternative attributes in the XACML requests; moreover, in order to allow the Visualization Component to extract and display arbitrary information from the logs, raw XACML requests are now also stored in the database [28].

The History-Based Assessment module is invoked by the PAC service bus (via topic subscription) whenever a citizen submits new answers to a questionnaire. It extracts a series of automatically-determined numerical features from the questionnaire answers and uses the LIONoso core library to predict the chance that an information processing request from the PA is rejected due to the citizen's privacy preferences, thus providing advice to the citizen with respect to his/her privacy choices. The predicted probability is stored in the citizen's PLA. This module is periodically re-trained with new information about the request rejection rate obtained by the notification module. This module is fairly independent from the other components, and no substantial modifications have occurred since its documentation in D3.5 [28].

The Law-Compliance Module is tasked with examining the PA's self-assessed compliance with national and EU privacy laws. A PA user is required to answer a PA-only self-assessment questionnaire with closed-form questions related to the fulfillment of specific criteria. All questions have a yes/no/not-applicable answer and are tagged with metadata detailing which answer is compliant. The law-compliance module scans the PA's questionnaire answers and generates a report containing all non-compliant answers. The report is attached to all PLAs in the PA part, so that every citizen is informed of any possible shortcoming in their sensitive information treatment.

Finally, a web module is exposed for configuration and to provide some real-time functionality, e.g., to perform an immediate log scan in addition to the periodic ones. All LIONoso functions, in fact, can only be accessed by PA users.

Privacy Agreement Enforcer (PAE)

The PAE, as part of the PRTC has had to adapt to the changes required by other tools as well as to changes required by the use case partners. With respect to the initial implementation PAE has been reworked to allow for a different management of how it uses the metadata on the questionnaire provided by DAE. Now PAE provides the means to configure which metadata keys it will search for in the questionnaire in order to use them for the generation of policy. This will allow the PAs to potentially use any kind of metadata keys they want.

In the same vein of providing a more complete generation of policies the PAE has been improved to be able to use more types of questions from the questionnaire.

There have been several minor improvements related to bug fixing and some related to specific functionalities, for example in the initial version when generating policies from questions of the type *date* the XACML policies used the data type *dateTime* while now they simply use *date*, which is more realistic.

Media Network Aware Element (MANE)

MANE applies Deep Packet Inspection (DPI) for packet filtering at both the network and the application layer. MANE is extended to accept and parse VisiOn privacy policies. The modification of the MANE according to the VPP requirements are:

- Initially, MANE was providing a web-based dashboard and the PA user would have to independently access the tool for getting information. in order to support the authentication mechanism of the VPP, MANE was integrated in the Visualization Tool (ViTo) and now is offered to the end-user with administrative rights, within the Web Framework GUI. This is more user-friendly and makes the tool more unified with the rest of the platform.
- Integration with Pilot applications and PAE: MANE handles real-time network traffic, so it can be considered as a tool that will work and be tested when everything is up and running, including both: the pilot application and the Web Framework. By performing tests, minor modifications had to be done in the exchanged XACML data, so as to make the flow of information work correctly. The outcome indicates that the correct privacy rules were being stored by MANE and later used and applied while handling user requests for resources.

3.3   Privacy Specification Component

The Privacy Specification Component (PSC) contains different tools with several functionalities. We previously described its privacy analysis functionality using the CARiSMA tool within the desktop framework. In this section, we introduce the Data Value Tool (DVT).

Data Value Tool (DVT)

The DVT identifies the most important and valuable information in the VPP. To integrate the DVT into the web framework, several modifications and integrations are performed:

- **Integration with DAE:** The first item in place was the integration with DAE. Main functionality of DVT is the calculation of the data value based on the perspective of the users. To do so, users are asked to fill a questionnaire which is analyzed in order to provide the necessary visualizations. To this end, a template questionnaire was provided and the DVT was updated to follow the data structure of DAE.

- **Integration with the VisiOn DB:** As mentioned above, DVT uses questionnaires and the user response to calculate the required values. All the communication takes places through the VisiOn DB where DVT reads the citizen answers, the PA's answer as well as the common PLA document and updates them after all calculations are complete.
- **Integration with authentication mechanism:** DVT uses always the currently logged user in order to provide the visualization, a small integration to pass the user was required.
- **Integration with ViTo:** ViTo is the main component for the visualization of the whole VisiOn Web Framework. Hence, DVT is integrated in ViTo as part of the whole framework. The integration includes the possibility of localization of DVT to different languages which is passed as an option from ViTo.
- **Revision to work with any questionnaire:** Finally, we require that citizens and PA need to answer a specific questionnaire for DVT. Nonetheless and to ease the work of the pilots and the overall user experience, DVT was updated to be able to read any questionnaire of DAE as long as specific metadata values are included.

3.4   Privacy Visualization Component (PVC)

The PVC provides a user interface to the citizens and PAs.

Visualization Tool (ViTo)

The Visualization Tool (ViTo) has been specifically developed for the project. It provides a web interface for the citizen and for the PA user.

The basic authentication method via username/password credentials has been replaced by a delegated authentication system. This required the removal of the previous authentication method and the replacement of user and role identification methods. All access to the ViTo interface is now regulated through the reverse proxy described. Following the introduction of the delegated authentication system, the user registration interface has been removed from the system. The web interface had been written in English and was not prepared for internationalization. Feedback from the use-case partners suggested that localization in the various national languages of the project partners is fundamental. Therefore, the ViTo code has been extended in order to be fully localized, and the use-case partners have been involved in the translation project.

In order to expose a more appealing interface to the user, the web pages is restyled with Twitter's Bootstrap framework, which has been considered mature and stable enough for a production environment. The ViTo contains an improved Notification display with the capability to define custom columns of application-specific interest. Moreover, ViTo provides an access to the MANE console.

4   Related Work

In literature, there are several approaches to support model-based security analysis. Some of those are summarized and discussed by Lano et al. [14]. A model-based use of security patterns has for example been addressed by Katt et al. and Nguyen et al. [13,17]. Further research makes use of aspect-oriented modeling for model-based security [6]. Heitmeyer et al. propose the application of formal methods on minimal state machine models for security verification [7].

Similar to CARiSMA, SecureUML provides a role-based access control using UML models [15]. While CARiSMA provides interfaces for adding arbitrary profiles and checks, SecureUML is limited to access control.

Security risk analysis can be performed with the CORAS tool [4]. In contrast to CARiSMA, CORAS works on proprietary models and uses the CORAS language, which was originally a UML profile but later defined as a domain specific language.

In [3], the authors benefit from the privacy analysis provided by CARiSMA, and introduce a privacy impact assessment supported by system models. They propose a set of security and privacy controls to mitigate the identified privacy risks.

Islam et al. integrated the Secure Tropos approach with UMLsec [9], to support the alignment of secure software engineering with legal regulations. However, this work does not support privacy requirements and they do not analyze security requirements to automatically perform appropriate UMLsec checks.

In [12], the authors propose an approach (PriS) for incorporating a user's privacy requirements into a system design. PriS provides a methodological framework to analyze the effect of privacy requirements on organizational processes. The authors focus on the integration between high-level organizational needs and IT systems. A privacy analysis is not conducted on a system model which expresses the behavior and the structure of a system.

In [26], an extension of privacy agreement levels by implementing access purposes for individual personal information in a lattice structure is introduced. This approach enables service customers to control the use of individual data. However, in this approach no privacy analysis regarding customer preferences is performed.

5   Conclusion

In this chapter, we provided a high-level architecture of the VPP and described the two main frameworks of the VPP according to the tools that are integrated into the VPP. Relying on the model-based methodologies, we described how privacy and security requirements of the public administrations may be modeled. Furthermore, using the SecTro tool, we explained how the identified security and privacy requirements can be satisfied by specific appropriate mechanisms. Moreover, SecTro enables the software engineers to model privacy threats and reason about how a system may be protected against such threats. Using CARiSMA, we illustrated the process of analyzing the behavior and the structure of a system model with UML diagrams. Such an analysis enables one to identify privacy and security violations of a system design, particularly in the early phases of the system development. We described the... .

Acronyms

PA	Public Administration
PLA	Privacy Level Agreement
VPP	VisiOn Privacy Platform
PET	Privacy Enhancing Technology
UML	Unified Modelling Language
STS-ml	Socio Technical Security - modelling language
SecBPMN2	Secure Business Process Modelling Notation 2.0
SecBPMN2-ml	SecBPMN2-modelling language
SecBPMN2-Q	SecBPMN2-Query language
IDS	Intrusion Detection System
CSB	Communication Service Bus
DPI	Deep Packet Inspection
PAC	Privacy Assessment Component
PSC	Privacy Specification Component
PRTC	Privacy Run-Time Component
PVC	Privacy Visualization Component
VDB	VisiOn DataBase
DAE	Dynamic Audit Engine
DVT	Data Value Tool
ViTo	Visualization Tool
PAE	Privacy Agreement Enforcer
STS-Tool	Socio Technical Security-Tool
MANE	Media Network Aware Element

References

1. Ahmadian, A.S., Strüber, D., Riediger, V., Jürjens, J.: Model-based privacy analysis in industrial ecosystems. In: Anjorin, A., Espinoza, H. (eds.) ECMFA 2017. LNCS, vol. 10376, pp. 215–231. Springer, Cham (2017). https://doi.org/10.1007/978-3-319-61482-3_13
2. Ahmadian, A.S., et al.: Model-based privacy and security analysis with CARiSMA. In: Proceedings of 2017 11th Joint Meeting of the European Software Engineering Conference and the ACM SIGSOFT Symposium on the Foundations of Software Engineering, pp. 989–993, September 2017. https://doi.org/10.1145/3106237.3122823
3. Ahmadian, A.S., et al.: Supporting privacy impact assessment by model-based privacy analysis. In: Proceedings of the 33rd Annual ACM Symposium on Applied Computing, SAC 2018, Pau, France, April 09–13, 2018, pp. 1467–1474 (2018)
4. den Braber, F., et al.: Model-based security analysis in seven steps–a guided tour to the CORAS method. BT Technol. J. **25**(1), 101–117 (2007). https://doi.org/10.1007/s10550-007-0013-9. ISSN: 1573-1995

5. Dalpiaz, F., Paja, E., Giorgini, P.: Security Requirements Engineering: Designing Secure Socio-technical Systems (2015). To appear
6. Georg, G., et al.: An aspect-oriented methodology for designing secure applications. INFSOF **51**(5), 846–864 (2009)
7. Heitmeyer, C.L., et al.: Applying formal methods to a certifiably secure software system. IEEE Trans. Softw. Eng. **34**(1), 82–98 (2008)
8. Hoepman, J.-H.: Privacy design strategies. In: Cuppens-Boulahia, N., Cuppens, F., Jajodia, S., Abou El Kalam, A., Sans, T. (eds.) SEC 2014. IFIP AICT, vol. 428, pp. 446–459. Springer, Heidelberg (2014). https://doi.org/10.1007/978-3-642-55415-5_38
9. Islam, S., Mouratidis, H., Jürjens, J.: A framework to support alignment of secure software engineering with legal regulations. Softw. Syst. Model. **10**(3), 369–394 (2011)
10. JDSoftware Inc. JDeSurvey repository on GitHub (2018). https://github.com/JD-Software/JDeSurvey. Accessed 18 May 2016
11. Jürjens, J.: Secure Systems Development with UML. Springer, Heidelberg (2005)
12. Kalloniatis, C., Kavakli, E., Gritzalis, S.: Addressing privacy requirements in system design: the PriS method. Requir. Eng. **13**(3), 241–255 (2008). https://doi.org/10.1007/s00766-008-0067-3
13. Katt, B., Gander, M., Breu, R., Felderer, M.: Enhancing model driven security through pattern refinement techniques. In: Beckert, B., Damiani, F., de Boer, F.S., Bonsangue, M.M. (eds.) FMCO 2011. LNCS, vol. 7542, pp. 169–183. Springer, Heidelberg (2013). https://doi.org/10.1007/978-3-642-35887-6_9
14. Lano, K., Clark, D., Androutsopoulos, K.: Safety and security analysis of object-oriented models. In: Anderson, S., Felici, M., Bologna, S. (eds.) SAFECOMP 2002. LNCS, vol. 2434, pp. 82–93. Springer, Heidelberg (2002). https://doi.org/10.1007/3-540-45732-1_10
15. Lodderstedt, T., Basin, D., Doser, J.: SecureUML: a UML-based modeling language for model-driven security. In: Jézéquel, J.-M., Hussmann, H., Cook, S. (eds.) UML 2002. LNCS, vol. 2460, pp. 426–441. Springer, Heidelberg (2002). https://doi.org/10.1007/3-540-45800-X_33
16. Mouratidis, H., Giorgini, P.: Secure tropos: a security oriented extension of the tropos methodology. Int. J. Software Eng. Knowl. Eng. **17**(02), 285–309 (2007)
17. Nguyen, P.H., et al.: SoSPa: a system of security design patterns for systematically engineering secure systems. In: MoDELS 2015, pp. 246–255 (2015)
18. OMG. BPMN 2.0. OMG (2011). http://www.omg.org/spec/BPMN/2.0
19. OMG. Unified Modeling Language (OMG UML). Technical report 2.5.1. Object Management Group (2017)
20. Pavlidis, M., Islam, S.: SecTro: a CASE tool for modelling security in requirements engineering using secure tropos. In: CAiSE Forum, pp. 89–96 (2011)
21. Pavlidis, M., Mouratidis, H., Islam, S.: Modelling security using trust based concepts. Int. J. Secure Softw. Eng. (IJSSE) **3**(2), 36–53 (2012)
22. Pavlidis, M., et al.: Dealing with trust and control: a meta-model for trustworthy information systems development. In: 2012 Sixth International Conference on Research Challenges in Information Science (RCIS), pp. 1–9. IEEE (2012)
23. Pavlidis, M., et al.: Modeling trust relationships for developing trustworthy information systems. Int. J. Inf. Syst. Model. Des. (IJISMD) **5**(1), 25–48 (2014)
24. Salnitri, M., Paja, E., Giorgini, P.: Maintaining secure business processes in light of socio-technical systems' evolution. In: RE Conference Workshops, pp. 155–164. IEEE (2016)

25. Salnitri, M., et al.: STS-tool 3.0: maintaining security in socio-technical systems. In: Proceedings of CAiSE Forum 2015, pp. 205–212 (2015)
26. van Staden, W., Olivier, M.S.: Using purpose lattices to facilitate customisation of privacy agreements. In: Lambrinoudakis, C., Pernul, G., Tjoa, A.M. (eds.) Trust-Bus 2007. LNCS, vol. 4657, pp. 201–209. Springer, Heidelberg (2007). https://doi.org/10.1007/978-3-540-74409-2_22
27. The Free Software Foundation, GNU Affero General Public License Version 3 (2007). http://www.gnu.org/licenses/agpl-3.0.de.html
28. VisiOn Project. D3.5 - Privacy Run-Time Component. Technical report (2016)

Empirical Evaluation of the VisiOn Privacy Platform

Dimitri Bonutto[1]([✉]), Ilia Christantoni[2], Dimitris Kosmidis[2],
Francesco Micucci[3], and Mattia Salnitri[4]

[1] Ospedale Pediatrico Bambino Gesu', Piazza Sant'Onofrio, 4, 00165 Rome, Italy
dimitri.bonutto@opbg.net
[2] DAEM S.A., Liosion 22, 10438 Athens, Greece
{i.christantoni,d.kosmidis}@daem.gr
[3] Ministero dello Sviluppo Economico, Via Molise 2, 00187 Rome, Italy
franco.micucci@mise.gov.it
[4] Politecnico di Milano, Via Ponzio 34/5, 20133 Milan, Italy
mattia.salnitri@polimi.it

1 Introduction

While previous chapters of this book describe the components and the architecture of the VisiOn Privacy Platform (VPP), this chapter focuses on its evaluation.

Evaluation is a central activity in any software development life cycle since allows to verify if requirements, defined for the software, are satisfied. We evaluated the VisiOn Privacy Platform (VPP) with empirical experiments on different domains, in order to evaluate the performance of the platform with different stakeholders and in different contexts. In particular, we selected three domains where sensitive/personal data and privacy are key factors; we integrated the VPP in existing Public Administration (PA) information systems and we evaluated the main aspects of the platform recruiting Public Administration (PA) employees and citizens.

The objectives of such experiments are not limited to the evaluation, they also aimed to advertise the platform to both citizens and PA employees, and to raise awareness towards the value of (sensitive) data and privacy in general.

The selected domains are:

- health care: two hospitals Ospedale Pediatrico Bambino Gesu' (OPBG) and Hospital Infantil Universitario Niño Jesus (HIUNJ) evaluated VPP in a cross border telemedicine scenario;
- municipality: DAEM, a company that manages the Athens' services to citizens, evaluated the VPP in a scenario where citizens use services of the city;
- tax refund: the Italian ministry for the economic development (MiSE) evaluated VPP in a scenario where companies request tax refund.

The rest of the chapter is organized in three sections where each empirical experiment is described in detail, and in a final, concluding, section. The data set of the empirical experiments for the three domains is freely available [16].

© Springer Nature Switzerland AG 2020
M. Salnitri et al. (Eds.): Visual Privacy Management, LNCS 12030, pp. 109–148, 2020.
https://doi.org/10.1007/978-3-030-59944-7_5

2 Evaluation Within a Health Care Domain

In the healthcare sector, medical devices and clinical systems must communicate in order to safely fulfill an intended purpose. Health Information Technology experts should be proficient in many areas, including the manner in which they organize and deliver services. Moreover, they should develop guidelines for individual clinical scenarios that define specific requirements for quality of services, clinical effectiveness, patient safety and cost effectiveness.

Telemedicine is the use of telecommunication and information technology to provide clinical health care remotely. The American Telemedicine Association's (ATA) definition of telemedicine is "the use of medical information exchanged from one site to another via electronic communications to improve a patient's clinical health status" [3]. Although the terms telemedicine, telehealth and eHealth are often used interchangeably, telemedicine applies more broadly to general health care, such as patient education and monitoring. The services are provided in several modalities: a) real-time, or synchronous, communication as telephone, Webcam, or audio or video links; b) the storage and forwarding of information, such as diagnostic-imaging data; c) remote patient monitoring, such as at-home vital sign measurement of blood glucose level testing; d) mHealth, which can include the use of wearable devices, cell phones, or smartphone applications [4]. Telemedicine involves medical data transactions of text, sound, and images, among others, in order to guide the prevention, diagnosis, treatment and follow-up of patients, as procedures. The information managed by a telemedicine platform are not only clinical data but in some cases also demographics data and questionnaires. The tasks supported by this technology could be more complex than those described above, for example data exchange with Electronic Health Record (EHR), follow-up visits schedule, ePrescription, eConsent and educational activities for the patient. Although telemedicine must be treated as any diagnostic/therapeutic health service, it does not replace a face-to-face medical encounter, which however can be enhanced by telemedicine transactions.

In this complex context, eHealth networks require technical teams to run the systems, and the Information Technology (IT) staff is almost completely independent to clinical staff and users. This presents privacy and security challenges by increasing the number of people other than the clinical staff with potential access to patients' records. Also, electronic transmission of information is always susceptible to breaches of privacy. Recent episodes have been reported by the media regarding hacker attacks to electronic systems of hospitals with high risks in terms of privacy and confidentiality. In a large scale, the healthcare domain is even more exposed to data breaches than other sectors and in many cases attacks could affect not only PCs but also more specialist equipment connected to hospitals networks, such as medical devices. Since IT is pervasive, easily available at any level and allows the transmission of every kind of data at practically no time, patients and physicians' inclination is to use every kind of telehealth product even without complying neither with security policies, nor with privacy protection conditions. The potential data transfer performed with no precautions concerning privacy protection, with unsecured tools like messaging mobile applications or electronic mail with no encryption or signature and even across borders is worrying. The success of telemedicine could be undermined if privacy, confidentiality and security risks are not addressed by the healthcare providers. If the proper technical steps are not taken both physicians and patients will lack trust in the use of eHealth solutions. Such trust is built on good patient-physician communication and contributes to improved treatment adherence and continuity of care [7]. Furthermore, healthcare facilities want to prove themselves accountable and transparent to patients and third parties like regulators and certified entities and to do so they must implement strong privacy and security policies.

Privacy risks of eHealth involve a lack of controls on the collection, use and sharing of sensitive personal information. Data use and disclosure is largely determined by technology companies with few legal boundaries for individuals to control the information flow [8]. Patients currently regulate who can access their personal health information through the compilation of an informed consent. The consent gives participants appropriate knowledge of what data are being collected, how they are stored and used, what rights they have to the data and what the potential risks of disclosure could be [2]. The necessity for the privacy-enabled management of personal data is reflected in the transition from paper-based health records to EHRs, that makes data exposed in the eHealth environment vulnerable to security and privacy threats, and in the GDPR, which aims to protect the data subjects' interests imposing data controllers to ensure data subjects' privacy and providing them the ownership and control of their data. OPBG and HIUNJ evaluated the VisiOn Privacy Platform (VPP) during a cross boarder data exchange. A telemedicine application must be integrated to the VPP to offer a complete eHealth service that achieves privacy management objectives applying Privacy by Design principles.

In the current context the privacy and security measures are established by national rules and the applications in IT systems are compliant with national rules. Furthermore, there is no central management control on privacy and security issues, most of the telemedicine platforms are from US (regulatory differences compared to EU), there is no control or detection of privacy issues in European Union (EU) telemedicine services, physicians and patients use improper communication instruments as phone call, e-mail, Skype and WhatsApp. Through the VPP we expect to provide a standard platform for analysis and enforcement of privacy and security, to be compliant with European regulation, to raise awareness of end users on privacy and security issues making them the main actors in managing their personal data and to integrate the informed consent for data transactions through the VisiOn online questionnaire.

2.1   Empirical Experiment Settings

There are many real-life context in which a doctor could access some of the health data of a citizen beyond the borders of his country. Some of the scenarios that the personnel of a hospital, namely a pediatric hospital, can recognize are:

- a patient has a complex and rare disease and the medical staff in charge of his follow up ask for a teleconsultation to a specialist group in another hospital to define the most appropriate diagnostic procedures and therapy;
- the patient has a chronic disease and is followed up by a third level hospital (a hospital that provides tertiary care, which is health care from specialists in a large hospital after referral), while travelling abroad he has a reactivation of his disease and he needs to perform a televisit with a doctor of the medical staff in charge of his follow up;
- a pediatric patient with a rare disease moves to another European country with his family and needs to transfer his clinical data in order to allow the hospital in the new location appropriately follow him up.

These scenarios are called respectively Teleconsultation, Televisit and Clinical Data Transfer. The scenarios have been modeled to work in an environment as much realistic as possible, using a web application by means of which the medical staff of one hospitals could retrieve the data from the web server of the other facility (a store and forward telehealth application). In order to show the benefits of the VPP, we decide to use a more straightforward process foreseeing a data retrieve in only one direction for every scenario involved in the pilot.

According to the ethics policies, no real patients participated in the trials and the experiment should be performed in a separated network with a test environment. For the clinical cases, a fictitious patient is being created, composed by different clinical data from different real patients affected by type 1 Neurofibromatosis and fictitious personal data. The clinical data is anonymous, so it is not be possible to lead to the patients' identity. The questionnaires of the empirical process was distributed and filled in an anonymous manner. The VPP platform did not know the real names of the children involved, neither indirectly. A table was held in the premises to assign each user in the VPP a unique integer number. There are two types of consents to be provided by the participants. Both consents were drafted in the language of each country, Italian and Spanish, and was followed the current formal standards in each hospital. One first consent form was presented at the time of recruiting and another at the beginning of each trial to the participants. We have created a factsheet in which we explain what is the purpose of the experiment, what are the benefits and risks of the project and the rights of the person according to the privacy national legislation. The consent is valid only if it is expressed freely in reference to a clearly identified and understandable treatment.

The request was generated by a doctor when he asks for a document on the web application database manager in the other country, this request was checked against the policies on the platform. The policies were created after the questionnaires has been filled up by the parents or the tutors of the ill children. The request contains information about the person or institution that asks for the health data, the identification number of the fictitious patient and the items that can be susceptible of privacy protection. The VPP compares the fields in the request to the privacy preferences that are recorded in that moment. The questionnaire is recorded in the VisiOn database and can be modified, any time the parents or tutors wish to.

During the pilot we have three types of users:

- hospital administrators (PA personnel) in charge of the modelling of the overall system;
- doctors (PA personnel) who connect to a web application to access the health data of a child with a particular illness according to the specialty of the doctor;
- parents and tutors as citizens that connect to VPP tools to declare their permissions to let the doctors of another EU country to access or not the health data of their children.

In the trials with hospital administrators (data controller) these steps are implemented:

1. welcome and explanation of the trial with a video and a leaflet;
2. reading and signing of a consent to participate the trial;
3. explanation of the VPP desktop tools through a short paper that explains the most important features of each application;
4. implementation of a VPP session during which the administrator can model a simple scenario and investigates the functionalities of the tools supported by the VisiOn project staff.

During design-time, the data controller and processor use VPP to capture security and privacy requirements of their systems by modelling and analyzing the system itself from different perspectives:

- the socio-technical environment of the hospital's system is captured by models of interactions between actors. These models capture goals the actors try to achieve and information/documents that are processed to achieve the goals (the security needs that can be specified for the transmission of a document are: integrity, anonymity, authentication, confidentiality, undetectability, and unlinkability);
- procedural models of business processes, enriched with security related information;
- potential threats to the hospital's systems and its environment that lead to security and privacy issues are captured and countermeasures to mitigate these risks are identified;
- trust relationships between the healthcare facility and third party providers are modelled and analyzed in order to realize whether these relationships endanger transparency and accountability from patients' parents perspective;
- once the requirements, with a special focus on the security and privacy aspect, are captured, the data controller's/data processor's system designer can specify the details of the system under planning, by using a standard modelling language.

Along with the models define above, privacy and security constraints on such models can be defined and verified. The results of such verification can be used by the system designers to refine and enhance the models in order to to meet privacy specifications.

In the trials with citizens (data subject) acting as parents of an ill child these steps are implemented:

1. welcome and explanation of the trial (in person, with a video and/with a leaflet);
2. reading and signing of a consent to participate in the trial;
3. implementation of a VPP session during which the citizens connect via web to fill the VisiOn questionnaires where they define and update their privacy preferences, stressing that they are giving permission for the data to be accessed from the hospital in the other country;
4. evaluation of the use of the Web Framework's tools and the general concept of the whole project through a questionnaire.

The privacy preferences are inputs to data access policies and PLAs. Data subjects can view their personal PLA, which furthermore contains visual representation of the systems involved in the processing of the data subjects' data, and the results of system analysis and law compliance checks performed by the data controller. Moreover, VPP provides useful insights to the data subjects regarding the value of their personal data. Finally, VPP enables data subjects to monitor issued access requests related to their personal data, the data access decisions and enforcements. The VisiOn online questionnaire, integration of the consent form for data transactions, is divided in three sections:

- "Patient Profile", in which we want to evaluate the level of computer expertise of the users and if they use periodically e-health services;
- "Privacy and Security aspects", in which we want to evaluate if users know the main privacy and security measures related to their sensitive health data;
- "Data Transmission aspects", in which the users can choose and set up which documents are accessible, for what purposes (i.e. emergence, specialized consultation and research) and the timeframe in which the information are retrievable from an external facilities' medical staff.

The evaluation questionnaire collects feedbacks on demographic features of the sample in study, usability, graphic appearance and perception of awareness on different privacy and security aspects before and after the empirical experiment.

Table 1. Demographic aspects of the population in study (N = 190)

Question	Options	OPBG		HIUNJ	
		%	N	%	N
Sex	Male	51.7	46	45.5	46
	Female	48.3	43	54.5	55
Age	20–29	9.0	8	31.7	32
	30–39	66.3	59	22.8	23
	40–49	14.6	13	14.9	15
	50–59	5.6	5	22.8	23
	≥60	4.5	4	7.9	8
Qualification	Bachelor	57.3	51	59.4	60
	Upper secondary	37.1	33	34.7	35
	Lower secondary	5.6	5	5.0	5
	Primary	0	0	1.0	1
Profession	Freelance	33.7	30	12.9	13
	Office worker	31.5	28	58.4	59
	Retired	6.7	6	3.0	3
	Student	5.6	5	14.9	15
	Unemployed	1.1	1	6.9	7
	Other	21.4	19	4.0	4

2.2   Results

Most of the subjects recruited for the pilot, simulated patients' parents or legal guardians (a more in-depth analysis of the sample will be developed in the following section). We recruited fewer administrators, who performed the empirical experiment using VisiOn desktop tools, since it was difficult to find in the hospital personnel who are simultaneously familiar with the concepts of digital health, privacy and security. In the first case, the hospitals personnel have collected quantitative results, while in the second case, having a very small sample size, we have focused on qualitative results.

In Table 1 we can see the demographic data extraction from OPBG and HIUNJ end users. The main differences are: a) OPBG staff recruited more people between the ages of 30 and 39 while HIUNJ staff recruited more people between the ages of 20 and 29 and 50 and 59; b) OPBG staff recruited more freelance worker while HIUNJ staff recruited more students and office workers. The difference between the percentage of male and female users is minimal, consequently, the study's sample is gender balanced. The sample being studied is gender balance. Almost 60% of the users are between the ages of 30 and 49. Very few people are over 60. About 94% of the users have at least a high school diploma. Nearly half of the users have a job as office worker while nearly 25% of

Table 2. Citizens evaluation questionnaire results

ID	Question	% Strongly agree	% Agree	% Neutral	% Disagree	% Strongly disagree
6	Are the information provided for the test by the OPBG/HIUNJ staff understandable?	31.6	34.2	17.9	12.1	4.2
7	Are the questions you answered on the VisiOn platform understandable?	18.9	36.8	20.5	15.8	7.9
8	Are loading times while browsing on the site reasonable?	25.8	53.7	17.9	2.1	0.5
9	Is the VisiOn web-site easy to use?	23.7	49.5	25.8	1.1	0
10	Does the application show a nice graphic appearance?	22.6	35.3	31.6	10.5	0
11	Before the empirical experiment did you know the main privacy and security aspects of health data?	6.3	15.8	35.3	34.2	8.4
12	Do you think this test has made you aware of the of privacy issue in the healthcare scenario by providing you with greater awareness and understanding of the importance of protecting your data?	17.4	46.3	18.9	13.7	3.7
13	Do you think VisiOn allows patients greater control over privacy using constraints on health data transmission?	23.7	49.5	14.7	7.4	4.7
14	Do you think VisiOn is an educational tool on data property and data accessibility only by authorized personnel issues?	32.6	46.8	14.7	4.7	1.1
15	Do you think the hospital can guarantee greater privacy while exchanging health data using VisiOn?	30.5	44.2	15.8	7.9	1.6
16	Do you feel this test has made you aware of the potential risks or benefits of consciously compiling the consent for the transmission of health data?	24.2	56.3	12.6	6.3	0.5
17	Do you think this platform can be useful for patients with particular clinical needs or problems such as reduced mobility?	31.1	42.1	18.4	7.4	1.1
18	Do you think the PLA offers a complete insight of VisiOn approach on privacy and security issues?	36.3	46.8	7.4	8.4	1.1

users are free professionals. Regarding the demographic section, the sample being studied has characteristics similar or at least coherent to those of the hospitals population.

Table 2 shows that two-thirds of the users said the information provided by the OPBG and HIUNJ staff to perform the empirical experiment was satisfactory (31.6 strongly agree - 34.2 agree). More than half of the users said that the questions about the VisiOn Web Framework were comprehensible (18.9 strongly agree - 36.8 agree). Conversely, less than 25% of users found the questions not so much understandable. More than 75% of the citizens stated that loading times during navigation in the VisiOn web platform are satisfactory (53.7 agree - 25.8 strongly agree). About 75% of users said that the VisiOn website (questionnaire compilation, PLA visualization, and data access attempt verification) was easy to use. Nearly 60% of users claimed that the web site looks more than satisfactory.

Just over 20% of citizens said that they had adequate basic knowledge in the field of privacy and security of health data before the pilot's take-over. While more than 40% said they had relatively poor basic knowledge on these topics. Almost 65% of users said the test gave them more awareness of the importance of protecting their health data. Nearly 75% of the patients agree that a product like VisiOn can provide greater control over the transmission of health data. More than 75% of citizens think that VisiOn is an educational tool also on data property issues and availability to access only authorized personnel. 75% of users think the hospital can guarantee greater privacy while exchanging health data using VisiOn. More than 80% of citizens is considered to be aware of the potential risks or benefits of a full-awareness compiling of the consent form for the transmission of health data. Over 80% of users think that the PLA approach offers a complete view from a technical point of view about the ongoing process during the controlled transmission of health data and information. Nearly 75% of citizens believes this platform can be useful for patients with particular needs or clinical problems.

We also wanted to verify the difference in the distributions for categorical variables, using the Pearson χ^2 test. The Pearson test mainly concerns the analysis of the distribution between the demographic variables that trace the patient profile with some following variables. One of the main points to consider consists in checking if age, gender, professions and school education can show different trends regarding users' perception on the VPP features (highlighted in the Q9-Q16 set of Questions). Through the statistical analysis described above we can state that there are no significant differences ($\rho > 0.05$) in trends if analyzed in terms of different gender, school education and profession (for this latter variable you may find slightly different trends but analyzing them nothing can suggest possible VPP improvements). If we analyze the different age groups we find that: a) younger users find that VPP is user friendly while, as the age advances, this perception decreases ($\rho < 0.01$); b) users between the ages of 30 and 39 are more receptive to VisiOn's features in particular awareness and understanding ($\rho = 0.026$), and VisiOn in data control during transactions ($\rho = 0.01$).

Finally, we used the Marginal Homogeneity Test to compare the perception on the general knowledge of privacy and security topics before the test and the knowledge in different specific features after the empirical experiment (Q11 vs. Q12-Q16). We have verified that patient's awareness on privacy and security topics improves once the test is performed. For example, if we compare Q11 with Q12: a) users who responded positively to Q11 are slightly over 20% while those who responded positively to Q12 are more than 65% (the trend is increasing); b) users who responded negatively to Q11 are more than 40% while the percentage is reduced to 15% when responding to Q12 (the trend is decreasing). This dynamic can also be verified by comparing Q11 with Q13-Q16. Apart from the quantitative feedback, the qualitative outcomes expressed by IT administrators while using the VPP Desktop Framework are also very useful. Most IT administrators believe that they need a more in-depth training to better utilize desktop applications but, despite a lack of basic knowledge of modeling languages such as UML, they have quickly adapted to the tools and think they can offer a good perspective for analyzing complex aspects of privacy and security intra and inter hospital.

2.3   Threats to Validity

A fundamental question concerning results from an experiment is how valid the outcomes are. It is important to consider the question of validity already in the planning phase in order to design the experiment ensuring adequate level of credibility for the experiment's results. In drawing conclusions we have four types, in each of which there is one type of threat to the validity of the results [19].

1. Conclusion validity. This validity refers to the relation between the treatment and the outcome. We want to make sure that there is a statistical relationship, i.e. with a given significance.
2. Internal validity. If a relation is observed between the treatment and the outcome, we must make sure that it is a causal relationship, and that it is not a result of a factor of which we have no control or have not measured. In other words that the treatment causes the outcome (the effect).
3. Construct validity. This validity refers to the relation between theory and observation. If the relation between cause and effect is causal, we must ensure two things: (i) that the treatment reflects the construct of the cause well and (ii) that the outcome reflects the construct of the effect well.
4. External validity. The external validity refers to generalization. If there is a causal relationship between the construct of the cause, and the effect, can the result of the study be generalized outside the scope of our study? Is there a relation between the treatment and the outcome?

Regarding the conclusion validity we have low statistical power due to limited number of users. We may have influenced the results by looking for specific outcomes (e.g. awareness, control over privacy, data property): this threat to validity is called "fishing". Two other possible threats are reliability of treatment implementation and random irrelevancies in experimental setting, in fact we can't control the environment of the users that participate in the experiment remotely despite we guide them through phone call. Regarding the heterogeneity of the subjects, we have chosen a sample indicative of the general patients' legal tutor or parents.

In terms of Internal validity, a possible threat could be *maturation*: subjects may react differently as time passed and, again, we don't have a full control over home based users. We assess this threat producing a restricted but essential number of questions so the users can learn the main topics of the project and, at the same time, not be tired and bored by the experiment itself. The selection threat is a delicate one: we recruited some users within the network of our contacts; this approach could lead to some forms of bias, in fact users may respond positively due to their direct knowledge with the examinator despite we suggest them to be as objective as possible.

Regarding the construct validity we have delivered to the users a document to explain the experiment and guide them through the whole process. In this way we have addressed the *inadequate preoperational explication of constructs* threat but we can't be sure that the home based users have read the document and that all the users were able to understand it. In terms of social threats we have the *hypothesis guessing* threat solved by creating a pretty clear and not ambiguous questionnaire, the *experimenter expectancies* threat that is not addressable because different users have probably different expectations and the *evaluation apprehension* threat that is not applicable to this experiment since there is no correct or incorrect answer to the questionnaire.

Regarding the external validity and in particular the *interaction of selection/setting and treatment* threats we have chosen a group of people assimilable to the general users of the hospital services, furthermore the patients' legal tutors can set up the PLAs only from home and from the hospital (supported by a physician) but there is not a perfectly working mobile version of the platform yet so the experiment can't be performed in every occasion as we initially supposed.

2.4   Discussions on the Empirical Experiment

VPP has proven to be a valuable application for the personal health information's privacy management. The users interpreting patients' parents were satisfied and their awareness on privacy aspects increased after the empirical experiment. In fact, the test was not done just to verify users' knowledge but also for training purposes. The questionnaire that the patients' parents compile on the VisiOn Web Framework explicitly refers to some key points of the privacy legislation that a curious user can further investigate. The answers were very encouraging considering that the privacy topic is not well known to the majority of the population. The results of the empirical experiment, however, shows that, if users are placed in a stimulating training environment such as trying out a personal data privacy management platform, the topic raises the general interest and fuels the desire to deepen apparently complex issues. In our opinion, the interest in this topic is growing above all in the health sector. Surely parents are mainly (and for good reason) interested and focused in the health of their children but they realize that an easy, fast and privacy-compliant access to health data for specialized physicians is an effective way and an added value in guaranteeing it.

IT experts, despite a lack of basic knowledge of modeling socio-technical systems, have quickly adapted to the desktop tools and think they can offer a good perspective for analyzing complex aspects of privacy and security. This holistic approach can also be a great opportunity for organizations to address specific requirements of the upcoming General Data Protection Regulation (GDPR) [11] and to implement e-consent solutions in their premises.

In the framework of European Union's laws, eHealth is considered a health and an Information and Communication Technologies (ICT) service so both regulations apply. However, the process of standardization is very difficult and some gaps at a national level may jeopardize a truly European market in healthcare services and slow the development of eHealth in Europe [14]. Concerning health services the most important achievement to regulate this domain is Directive 2011/24/EU (Cross-border directive) while in the ICT environment it must be taken into consideration especially the new GDPR.

The implementation of an e-consent solution is very difficult from a regulatory point of view. Consent is valid only if it is expressed freely, in reference to a clearly identified treatment and understandable (patient's awareness on the privacy policies). However, over reliance on consent too often results in weak privacy protections because patients frequently do not read or fully understand privacy policies. Technological and societal changes in information practices present fresh opportunities for innovative implementation of informed consent. Apps, tablets, video, interactive computers, robots, personal digital assistants, mobile phones and smartphones and wearable technology could help to modernize, alter, and improve methods of informed consent. Technologies permit broad standardization and easy updating of information and documentation of the process. Along with providing opportunities, adoption of digital and electronic methods of consent requires deliberation, evidence, and recognition of challenges. Investigators and oversight bodies must still determine the appropriate content for disclosure. Replacing long, complex, technical written forms with long, complex, technical or legalistic electronic information pages would not represent progress. Important additional challenges in digital consent interactions include verifying that the people who are consenting have the capacity to consent and are who they say they are (authentication). If informed consent aims to provide information that participants can use to make decisions, promoting informed consent will require the creative use of electronic technologies that are simple, easy to use, and in widespread and common use. The interactions need to be brief, engaging, informative about risks and benefits in a way that users can easily appreciate, and equipped with methods for authentication [6].

Another very important topic is the deployment method of the VisiOn service. OPBG installed the platform in an on-premise environment while HIUNJ in a cloud environment. Cloud technologies are very attractive in the healthcare sector, especially for their ability to reduce the costs of acquiring IT tools (hardware and software), maintenance, updating and the possibility of using services only when needed and in a totally flexible and scalable way. On the other hand, there are limitations in privacy and security that are not indifferent because the data are stored in servers that cannot be controlled by the hospitals and it is necessary to stipulate a Service Level Agreement with the cloud provider making sure that all security measures are respected. It is essential to clearly define the responsibilities of data controllers and data processors. The advantages and disadvantages are not limited to the aspects of costs and safety and in some scientific articles a rigorous study has been done regarding aspects of minor but important impact [9].

3   Evaluation Within a Municipality Domain

The empirical experiment in Athens questioned the usefulness and usability of VPP in terms of user confidence, when requested the delivery of an online service and at the same time assessed user trust to the interconnected municipal online system. The ultimate goal was to declare up to which level VPP facilitated data sharing and control and reduced user reluctance due to the perception of poor privacy assurance or process complexity. Moreover, the adoption of new eGovernment solutions is directly related to the ease-of-learning by end-users setting the ground for another factor under study.

Public Administration authorities are working towards upgrading the level of their online services through new governance models. This pushes for greater transparency, accountability and innovation, aiming at increasing citizen levels of confidence and trust in online services. In this context, user data privacy has become an important issue.

The VisiOn Privacy Platform (VPP) case scenario in Athens was built around a common transaction between a Citizen (C) and a City Authority/PA, namely the issuing of an official transcript of a Birth Certificate. "George's Story" was simulated through an empirical experiment, with primary focus on the "Security by Design" principle and its actual implementation into a legacy PA computer system, - the Municipality of Athens Computer System (MACS).

Security by Design, means that computer software is designed from the foundation to be secure. The obvious question which comes in mind and gets addressed through the DAEM empirical experiment is, what really happens when different software operates together in the City, how software components are interconnected and integrated, and how Municipal computer systems implement manual and/or offline processing in a consistent, reliable and trustworthy manner.

In the Athens empirical experiment, citizens were seen as empowered and engaged actors in the process, - actors who through their PLA, adequately address their privacy issues, - both online and offline. Through the experiment, citizens were entitled and prompted to issue, revise and revoke the terms of use of their personal data. They were given the practical means to manage their privacy concerns, before requesting public service(s) provided by the City of Athens (CoA). Within the same empirical experiment, the main challenge for the City Authorities was to emulate, through a popular and realistic scenario, the seamless operation and interoperability of its legacy systems, with third party software.

Based on an assumed degree of an ever-going digital transformation, and the trustworthiness of the implied service delivery by the PA at present time, DAEM questioned the business flow transparency, and the overall user accountability and responsibility during the process execution. The empirical experiment presented the framework, the principles, a toolbox and a model, for an End-2-End Service Design and Delivery, when it comes to accessing, processing and transmitting personal data by PA. The approach was based on the fundamental right of citizens to be informed regarding the management of their data, and their required consent for their personal data usage. The core idea was that citizens should be informed in a timely manner and be in-control of their own data in MACS, whilst PA should be held accountable for their own actions. Furthermore, the VPP approach in the Athens empirical experiment, aimed to strengthen digital human rights through the prevention of various types of data breach. Lastly, DAEM examined how VPP could possibly open new opportunities for developing innovative personal data-based services, built on mutual trust, through the provision of up-to-the-date indicators about the economic value of personal data.

3.1 Empirical Experiment Settings

The main challenge DAEM targeted to tackle through the implementation of the empirical experiment was the design and delivery of digital services not only in a prompt and efficient way but also based on identified citizen needs. DAEM as the main and oldest IT provider of the largest municipality in Greece has a long experience in the design and development of IT projects targeting both the public administration and the citizens as well. Through its long experience in service delivery, DAEM has repeatedly reported and encountered citizens' reluctance in using online services. Scaling up to the latter, the City of Athens has launched a promising Digital Strategy that DAEM shall facilitate.

Athens is constantly upgrading the digital capacity of its public services, with aim to better serve citizens and business, with results and transparency. Upgrading the municipality's computer systems and services is part of the agenda to transform Athens, into a "Smart City". Hence, Data Protection and Data Transparency is a milestone objective for the establishment of a trusted relation among PA and C. Citizen "proactive" engagement on the other hand is a mandatory and critical requirement for the development of services that aim to have a high level of penetration within the population.

The empirical experiment in Athens was built around a digital service delivery, which required the issuance of a Birth Certificate transcript for a citizen, using online Municipal facilities. George, a citizen and a city resident, is about to consume a municipal service and needs to prove his current residency status. An up-to-date transcript of his Birth Certificate will be the proof required by the service provider, which is a third-party organization associated to the City. George's Birth Certificate derives from the City Registry. In order for the transcript to be issued and transmitted, a Public Administrator must gain authorization so to access George's records and moreover, rights to process selected data. The City Registry is simulated as a component of the MACS.

The empirical experiment involves two main roles/actors, the Citizen (C) and the PA. They both communicate with MACS through computer interfaces. In the implemented scenario, when George (C) registers/logs into MACS through the Self-Service interface, he is prompted to issue/review the terms of use of his stored data. A small extra step enables the Privacy Level Agreement (PLA) mechanism within VPP. George is giving his consent regarding access and use of his personal data by the PA, answering a simple, yet comprehensive questionnaire. Upon the completion of the questionnaire, his PLA is being generated/updated. From this point onwards VPP will validate any PA request regarding service delivery and depending on George's answers to specific questions, VPP will either deny or grant authorization and the respected rights to the PA.

Scope of the Experiment

VisiOn Privacy Platform, facilitated the creation of a custom-made PLA by the citizen. This PLA was meant to be aligned with emerging European Law and Legislation and support below EU General Data Protection Regulation (GDPR) compliance. The platform was designed to be configured by PAs in order to monitor the level of law compliance, and to provide the necessary enforcement when the actual state would not meet the predefined agreement.

VPP introduced a Visual Privacy Management paradigm, which supported transparency and trust in PA actions, in three complementary ways:

1. the PA analyzed the service and developed the initial on-line version of the PLA, which was then shared with the citizen through the platform. George, visualised, modified and submitted his revised PLA, within the context of his own privacy needs, at the given time. His trust in MACS was meant to increase, by directly identifying how the PA will apply relevant privacy laws and regulations;
2. the PA analyzed the potential threats to George's specific privacy needs and defined the necessary countermeasures, so to minimize them;
3. the PA analyzed trust relationships with third party providers and established whether these relationships endangered the required transparency and accountability from the citizen's perspective.

Through George's story, DAEM emulated the use, control, processing and transmission, as well as personal data reuse, which impose major challenges for PA, MACS and their supporting infrastructure. The proposed Athens scenario aimed to address a wide number of rights that citizens are entitled to possess control, as indicatively mentioned below.

Citizen Rights:

- Right to know what personal information exists
- Right to see the actual content of personal information
- Right to rectify false personal information
- Right to audit who accesses and processes personal information and why
- Right to obtain personal information and use it "freely"
- Right to share or sell personal information to third parties
- Right to remove or "delete" personal information.

Moreover, the counter part of PAs test scenario scaled up to the additional enhancement of tasks.

PA Facilitating Activities:

- API implementation - no central infrastructure and control
- Citizen data aggregation
- Citizen consent handling: i.e., delegation, re-purposing

The modular approach of VPP within the Athens empirical example, leveraged the engagement of PA within the redesign process of a popular City Service and the support to coordinating activities, related to personal data use. The actual implementation, performed an initial needs analysis and design by the PA, -through the facilitation of the Desktop Framework toolbox, so to address George's privacy issues and to eliminate or minimize the impact of possible security vulnerabilities. The generated design model on privacy and data protection, was in accordance with the GDPR, and compliant with the "Security by Design" principle. Besides that, the empirical example attempted to ensure data security and process transparency through all phases of the City Service lifecycle.

Integration of VPP with MACS, was achieved through a series of parallel and interconnected activities. A number of design tool components of the VPP interface was utilized and the required link mechanisms were implemented, in an "almost realistic/hybrid-cloud" environment. In general, and due to its flexibility, the VPP solution proved to be agile and with potential to evolve according to fluid City needs and regulation changes.

Empirical Experiment Implementation

The empirical experiment integrates an OPANDA Front Desk application with MACS. OPANDA is the Cultural, Sports and Youth Organization of the City of Athens and in the VisiOn scenario acts as the third-party organization and service provider in George's story. Using the Front Desk application, a PA is able to administer programs and events, various kinds of subscriptions and citizens' service requests.

The simulated OPANDA application, handles multiple service requests in real-time. All citizens' requests are administered according to their status of residency, i.e., Athenians are eligible for certain discounts on program subscriptions and retain perks on services facilities. In the scenario executed, those later features are exploited through an OPANDA/MACS integration.

For the issuance of George's Birth Certificate transcript, and consequently the validation of his residency status, the request is initiated by an OPANDA front-desk officer, namely a PA. The data that must be accessed and processed by the (PA), include the unique national identifier. For the pilot scenario the unique identifier is AMKA, the Social Insurance Number that is issued for each citizen. Since the usage of George's stored AMKA is defined by him through his active PLA, service delivery will be either denied or allowed.

The empirical experiment was implemented in three (3) incremental pilot phases, with recurring tests, based on the degree of integration of the various software components, in order to simulate a realistic, up-to-date scenario and propose a complete technical solution. Figure 1 shows an overview of the implementation of the George's case study, used for the empirical experiment.

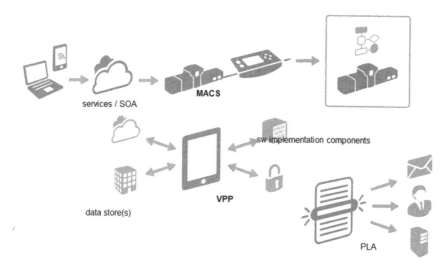

Fig. 1. Pilot schematic overview

3.2 Results

The coordinated trials engaged a total of more than 80 volunteers, who evaluated (a.) the concept, to generate their PLAs as part of the service delivery, and (b.) the ease of use of the procedure, when they were prompted to familiarize themselves with the PLA creation, through user-friendly questionnaire(s). The target group of end-users was guided to perform the pilot scenario in the scope of either the citizen or the PA.

The design, development and integration of the VPP from a technological point of view, has followed a systematic workflow, which identified a set of requirements, as success criteria. A similar process of requirements' definition and elicitation, formulated the evaluation approach, which assessed user perception, focused primarily on privacy, security and trust issues.

An online tool facilitated the gathering and export of quantitative results. These results were combined and further analyzed with qualitative outcomes, deriving from short interviews and discussions with participants mainly from the PA role. PA trials were executed in person, over an extended time period, which made possible the collection of anonymous testimonials and the elicitation of personal opinions, through open discussions. The latter included also a training/demonstration of the Desktop tools of VPP as well as the PA interface of the Web Framework, in order to familiarize PAs with the configuration of VisiOn Web Framework and in parallel demonstrate the potentiality of process modelling tools integrated in the VisiOn Desktop Framework.

Demographic Data

The sample of participants was equally distributed to male and female ranging from 18 to 41 years old with a majority of users in the age group of 30–40 (Fig. 2).

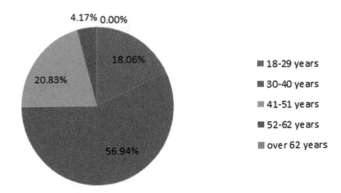

Fig. 2. Age-group distribution

The initial hypotheses under evaluation were addressed in the assessment questionnaire and the most important results are presented in the following sections categorized by factor. Table 3 reports the most significant questions with the results collected with the questionnaires.

Usefulness - Usability
The innovative services in the field of privacy offered through the VPP were assessed by the DAEM empirical experiment, with both citizens and PAs. Table 3 shows that approximately 85 % and 64 % respectively gave positive answers in the relevant questions, i.e., questions 1 and 2.

The usability of VPP in terms of UI/UX design received a high level of acceptance with over 70 % of positive answers by the users that tested the platform both on the citizens interface and administration interface (question 3).

Especially for the PA audience of the experiments, the advanced functionalities and administration features of VPP was evaluated as usable by approximately 70 % (question 4), although some qualitative feedback stated the need of technical competences acquisition by PAs in order to exploit the full potential of VPP, especially on process modelling activities.

Ease-of-Learning
Both PAs and citizens agreed with the perception that VPP is a technical solution easy to use and learn with the provision of use instructions and the execution of a request is an easy to learn task (questions 5,6, and 7).

Increased Perception of Privacy and Trust
The increased perception of privacy trust and security induced in public services by VisiOn platform was prominently stated by DAEM end-users both citizens and PAs (questions 8,9 10).

The audience of users recruited for the role of citizens in the pilot scenario provided a highly positive feedback of 80 % evaluating the PLA definition for the use of their personal data and the expend of assistance that VPP offered for PLA creation (question 11 in Table 3).

3.3   Threats to Validity

As analyzed in the previous sections, this empirical experimentation aimed to test the proposed approach by contacting real end-users (PAs and citizens) in order to evaluate it under the scope of its usefulness and usability. The rest of the session analyses the selection of subjects and the threat of validity.

Population of Interest

Since VisiOn approach refers to an ICT solution integratable to existing administration systems as an additional layer for data protection, the population of interest for evaluation is any stakeholder group involved in an electronic transaction system that offers services. In particular, Athens pilot targeted both citizens requesting eServices, as well as PAs handling the requests. Hence, the pilot experiment was designed to cover the full range of users within a public authority.

The volunteers engaged for the role of the citizens were real citizens that were guided to perform the pilot scenario while for the role of PA actual PAs were recruited. Part of the PA audience were also professionals in the field of IT, apart

Table 3. Most significant questions and their answers, of the questionnaire filled in by subjects after the empirical experiment execution.

ID	Question	Strongly agree	Agree	Neither agree or disagree	Disagree	Strongly disagree
1	The VPP is a very useful platform for providing innovative services to citizens, as far as privacy is concerned	22.22	62.50	15.20	0	0
2	The requested service was successfully completed with VPP	9.94	56.94	2778	8.33	0
3	I find the design of VPP nice	20.83	55.56	16.67	5.56	1.39
4	It is easy to understand the functionalities of VPP	18.92	51.35	24.32	5.41	0
5	I find VPP easy to use given that I have been provided with the relevant usage instructions	12.50	63.89	16.67	6.94	0
6	It is easy to learn how to use the VPP	19.44	50	16.67	12.50	1.39
7	I know how to complete a request in VPP	9.72	62.50	22.22	5.56	0
8	The VPP would improve privacy in public services provided to citizens	23.61	58.33	15.28	2.78	0
9	The VPP would increase trust to public services	25	51.39	22.22	1.39	0
10	VPP provides a secure service	12.50	63.89	22.22	1.39	0
11	VPP assists citizens regarding the preferred level of privacy	8.57	71.43	20.00	0	0

from the Municipality of Athens administrators and employees. Consequently, the experiment participants depicted a realistic segment of the population of interest for the VPP.

Conclusion Validity

Under conclusion validity, the *statistical power* of the pilot was not low, since a realistic pattern can be identified in the experiment's data. The outcomes as presented and analyzed quantitatively through the online evaluation survey, revealed a homogeneous trend in the results both during their initial analysis but also during the more specific clusterized research.

The *assumption of the statistical tests* foresaw the recruitment and engagement of sufficient number of end-users in order to participate in the experiment and provide feedback and evaluation. The target group finally included 87 participants that constituted a strong sample for the provision of an initial evaluation, not imposing consequently a threat to construction validity.

The main result that was targeted for evaluation was the increased perception of privacy and trust by the users, however a large number of other objectives and requirements were validated alongside during the project's pilots. Consequently, it can assumed that *fishing* is eliminated. Additionally, the cross-analysis of the results ensures a low *error rate* for the experiment.

The measures for the evaluation were foreseen to cover many different factors that could impose a risk on *reliability* e.g. the instrument used was an online open-access survey tool that offers increased potential on survey development, analysis of the results as well as a configurable UI. Hence, the layout and structure of the evaluation questionnaire was appropriately configured with user-friendly features such as paging, introduction and thank you message, background colours, project logos etc. The questions' wording and structure have been shared, approved and commented by the consortium ensuring the quality of all pilot surveys.

Threats to conclusion validity are introduced by the *experimental settings* since the pilot rounds were executed in diverse areas, environments and set-ups according to the targeted audience. Namely, some volunteers in the role of citizen were contacted personally through physical meetings and others via email. The PA participants followed an initial demonstration/training on the Desktop and Web VisiOn framework and its features for PAs, but the PA pilot rounds were executed in different frames and environments, e.g. internally in the premises of DAEM, in the Municipality of Athens, in external events etc.

The implementation of the pilot could not be characterized as standard although the project personnel put an effort to depict as homogeneous conditions and guidelines as possible. However, the different level of technical integration in each pilot round execution, the different means of contact with the participants and the diverse pilot settings introduce a threat in the *reliability of treatment implementation*.

The citizens volunteers were randomly contacted without targeting a particular profile of individuals. Also, the PA participants were mainly actual PAs of the Municipality and DAEM personnel, as well as professionals with an IT background. The technical implementation of VPP requires high IT skills and this restricted the initial preparation of the PA pilot and the experiment's assumption had to be updated. Despite that the analysis of the results depicts a generally *heterogeneous sample* in terms of gender, level of education and age provided that both citizens and PAs were by default adults at a working age.

Internal Validity

In the scope of internal validity, Athens pilot falls in the category of single groups since no control group was used. There is no threat regarding the *experiment history*, as the same object was not applied to a single individual twice.

During the Athens pilot the *maturation* and *testing* risks had already been predicted by the personnel and we had especially prepared a pilot implementation that would minimize negative effect during the execution. The goal was to perform a well-structured pilot that presents the innovative features of VisiOn. Additionally, all supporting material - both physical and electronic - was well designed and validated by the consortium to ensure high quality and eliminate threats from *instrumentation*.

The participants target group was not selected based on previous participation, since a similar pilot on data protection had not been executed before in DAEM. Part of the volunteers were randomly contacted in events with no prior participation in DAEM's projects and activities. This reveals that there was a natural variation in the audience and there no *selection risk* nor *statistical regression*.

The threat of sample *mortality* was especially present in the Athens pilot. There were in total 25 incomplete participations that were considered as dropouts, since they did not complete the pilot scenario execution as it was referred in the description/guidelines. A participation was considered complete in case all steps of the pilot were followed by the volunteers: consent - scenario execution - evaluation. The sample of drop-outs has not been analyzed yet.

Construct Validity

The majority of threats to construct validity under the category of *design threats* had been eliminated by default due to the project evolution, pilot tasks preparation and quality assurance of the pilots work package that detailly designed and prepared the pilot activities.

VisiOn theory has been efficiently described and transformed into testing scenarios even during the project proposal period, consequently, for each pilot the *pre-operational explication of constructs* was sufficiently represented in the scenario.

Moreover, there was no *interaction* of an individual in *different treatments* nor *interaction between testing and treatment*, since these were not applicable in the pilot design. Finally, the initial hypotheses to be tested and requirements to be validated were appropriately stated as main objectives of the pilot including specific parameters under testing. The objectives' diversity was wide and all important factors were subject to evaluation, consequently significant parameters have not been ignored. So, the constructs can be generalized without a risk of *restriction* across them.

Regarding the *social threats* to construct validity, the *hypothesis guessing* threat is unfortunately a factor that we assume that it was not completely eliminated. Most participants are positively inclined towards a research project and they naturally support its success. Hence, this threat was present in the DAEM pilot experiment as well. We mitigated this threat by being as neutral as possible, to avoid influencing the subjects, and by suggesting to the subject to be as objective as possible. This threat, however, had a positive impact in the *evaluation apprehension* since it was noticed that the pilot results did not include only positive quantitative results but important qualitative feedback and anonymous testimonials as well. The feedback referred to points of further improvement, additional preferred features for the evolution of VPP and useful comments on the VPP operation.

Finally, *experimenters' expectations* did not introduce a threat to construct validity of the results, since a segment of the pilot evaluation was performed remotely through email instructions and guidelines.

External Validity
The external validity of Athens pilot was mainly ensured during the preparation phase.

Participants were initially selected and contacted prior to the recruitment phase. The target groups included a representative sample for each pilot role and the description did not foresee the recruitment of individuals that were not appropriate for the experiment (e.g. under-aged, not Greeks, non-Athenians etc.). Moreover, the testing setting included appropriate tools since an actual eService system was used in the pilot that had been recently developed and operated within the Municipality. Finally, the tool for evaluation, as mentioned before, was an online open-access service. So the threats of *selection-treatment interaction* and *setting-treatment interaction* are not present.

The same applies for the threat of *history-treatment interaction* since there were no special events experienced during the pilot implementation.

The VisiOn project evaluation refers to the field of Applied Research, thus, as reported in Cook and Campbell, the priorities in validity threats are classified in descending order: internal, external, construct and conclusion. So the majority of threats, concentrated in the conclusion validity, are of less significance for the pilot results comparing to internal, external and construct validity where less threats are imposed.

3.4   Discussions on the Empirical Experiment

The Athens VisiOn pilot aimed to promote, demonstrate and communicate the scope of VisiOn proposed solution and to demonstrate the technical implementation of VPP and its features to public administrators and citizens in order to conduct an experimental trial for its assessment and evaluation. The criteria under evaluation were defined according to the specific needs of online administration systems deployed in municipal agencies aiming to provide services to citizens. Thus, the initial hypotheses under evaluation are usability, usefulness, ease-of-learning and the level of increased perception of privacy and trust after the technical integration of of VPP to existing eGovernment systems.

The experiment preparation included the formulation of an online survey following the evaluation methodology in order to check the fulfillment of the objectives. The experiment trials included recruited individuals volunteering participating on the role of citizens and public administrators of the municipality.

The perception of increased trust and privacy was validated by the vast majority of users and the innovative nature of VisiOn solution was evident. The outcomes of Athens use-case are amplified by the analysis of the experiment's possible validity threats that revealed a positive feedback regarding the experimentation process and the absence of major threats for the evaluation. A high potential on the application of VPP in services oriented to citizens was resulted since its usefulness and usability were appraised.

4   Evaluation Within a Ministry Domain

Public administration interacts every day with a large number of players, public or private entities, such as users, companies, stakeholders and other PAs. None of these interactions would be possible without a mandatory exchange of information as well as a minimum degree of mutual trust. The PA collects and stores information in many ways, especially through public utilities, which are increasingly involved in online services and databases. The law authorizes the PA, with some restrictions, to collect and store this huge amount of data, but there is an increasing demand for security and privacy, not only in terms of relations between PA and other actors, but also in terms of design and development of all those applications required to ensure appreciable standards of public services, through the optimization of infrastructures and technologies, in the perspective of a future *e-government*. This means also that software, in a public environment, should be designed with the purpose to harmonize it with the legislation and with the role of impartiality that the PA is called to perform in carrying out its official duties. Under the influence of such awareness, the best was to identify an application suitable for the purpose, namely an application able to bridge between the complexity of administrative processes and the real needs of citizens and companies aspiring to obtain services or funding from PA. VPP filled such gap, since it could be used to gather citizens' privacy needs and at the same time enforce them inside PA information systems.

Since the objective of our empirical experiment was to evaluate the VPP in a real PA environment, we decided to exploit "Credito d'Imposta Per l'Assunzione di personale Qualificato", transl.: "Tax credits for hiring skilled personnel" (CIPAQ), for its suitable characteristics. CIPAQ was in fact a service used by companies in order to receive a tax credit from MiSE, if certain conditions were met. In particular, companies had to submit a set of formal requirements (for approval), through an online procedure. More exactly, the main task of the case study consisted in recruiting skilled personnel, mostly employees with a high education and learning rate. The application CIPAQ was developed a couple of years before, as a web portal. The front-end was managed online by the application itself, the back-end, conversely, was managed by administrative and IT employees: the former examined the documentation, the latter were concerned with security and global functioning of IT infrastructures.

4.1 Empirical Experiment Settings

The empirical experiment was planned to gather information on the VPP, specifically: ease of use, intuitiveness, appearance and efficacy. In addition, it was designed to discover users' opinion about the platform, their awareness on privacy issues and security threats, the real perception they had of the CIPAQ platform, before and after the application of VPP. Data samples were collected, besides, according to specific schemes (gender, role, job, expertise, etc.).

Main objectives of the empirical experiment:

1. collecting feedback on users' privacy expectations;
2. rating the ease of use of the platform;
3. estimating the potential and the reliability of the VPP;
4. evaluating users' trust in its capabilities.

All this features are in accordance with MiSE's institutional objectives, first of all the promotion of industrial growth, and besides they can concretely support citizens and companies in the enforcement of *e-government*, through the development of online services, compliant with law and privacy standards. Thus, we formulated one or more hypotheses on how and if these objectives were concretely achieved. Were they achieved by adopting a specific method, following precise principles and implementing coherent actions? According to a Goal Question Metric (GQM) approach [17], we defined the experiment as shown in Table 4.

Table 4. GQM definition of the empirical experiment

Questions	Answers
What was studied? (object of study)	PA services and processes were studied
What was our intention? (purpose)	To evaluate whether services and processes met privacy requirements or not
What effects were supposed to be studied? (quality focus)	The benefits and the effectiveness deriving from a closer integration of the VPP into PA's online services and processes
Under whose point of view? (perspective)	Under the perspective of citizens and companies (users)
In what circumstances? (context)	In the context of online transactions between users and PA (e-Government)

In particular, 1st and 2nd questions specify the goals of the experiment, and refer to a more conceptual level, while 3rd, 4th and 5th questions describe the goals from an operational point of view, defining models, contexts, features and characteristics.

Description of the Case Study

CIPAQ, is a service that MiSE offers to companies and high qualified employees, so that they can benefit from tax discounts established by law and Italian government. We applied the VPP to such system and asked subjects who participated to the empirical experiment to use VPP functionalities within CIPAQ system, while playing the roles of PA users and/or companies (also called non-PA users).

CIPAQ has a complex structure, based on intensive interactions, that heavily involve the system and impact on privacy and security requirements of companies and that are closely related to constraints imposed by law. The main actors in the scenario are:

- **Companies**: they request a tax credit for the recruitment of highly qualified profiles;
- **MiSE**: MiSE is the main actor, who provides tax credit through the support of a skilled office and of the "Office Information Systems";
- **Office Information Systems**: it oversees the respect of specific Italian Laws on transparency, data storage and information management, according to privacy constraints;
- **Internal Domain**, composed of back-office operators: these operators inspect companies' claims, after completing an arrangement of checks, in order to allow, through data processing and regulatory strategies, the provision of the tax credit;
- **External Stakeholders** e.g., external investors, public or private subjects, citizens, etc., in other words, external parties interested in benefiting from CIPAQ data. Such role is included since, according to Italian law on digitalization, at the end of the case study data must be published without copyright restrictions (Open Data).

In order to receive tax credit, companies must disclose information on their recruitment of highly qualified personnel and fill out an online form provided by MiSE, which includes both data on the company, such as projects, activities, research, etc. and data on the recruitment, that is, number of employees, wages, professional skills and job roles. The authorization is granted at the end of the process, after that, MiSE must publish online, as required by Italian law on transparency, the overall amount of tax credit granted to the companies, along with other data and information.

This depicts an intricate system of relationships and interactions between MiSE and various partners, both inside and outside the Ministry, including different PAs. MiSE, for its institutional purpose, doesn't directly manage sensitive data, such as medical data or political and religious affiliation, however, during the above mentioned online procedure, relevant data clusters are submitted by companies to MiSE, with important economic and strategic implications.

This requires the creation and enhancement of a detailed PLA between MiSE, in the role of a Public Authority, and the companies, as recipients of public services.

CIPAQ is an excellent "case study", because it involves, in a fully functioning environment, multiple subjects, both public and private. Due to some critical issues, including legal constraints imposed by MiSE in its institutional role, it was necessary to plan a simulated scenario, with fictitious data and actors, in order to adapt it, under particular conditions and/or during specific tasks, to the structure of the VPP. However, the data crafted for the experiment were realistic and they did not influence the outcome of the case study.

For this reason, after the setup, the case study was partitioned into two different scenarios, the first dedicated to PA operators (also called PA users) and the second to anyone who might be interested in it (called non-PA users). However, although it may effectively seem that two different experiments were simultaneously conducted, the procedure can actually be considered as a unified experiment.

Experiment Phases

The experiment was articulated into two phases.

The first phase consisted in evaluating the level of trust and overall satisfaction of PA users towards the VPP. It was divided into two sub-phases. In the first one the Desktop Framework was used, while in the second the Web Framework. Specifically, the aim of the first sub phase was to evaluate the functionality and reliability of each software tool and to learn how to model scenarios according to users' privacy requirements. This goal was achieved through practical demonstrations and a tour of sessions addressed to MiSE operators, in order to make them aware of how the project architecture worked and, above all, to make them acquainted with all the innovations and improvements introduced within CIPAQ system. Then, in the second sub phase, subjects were asked to test the Web Framework, playing the role (and assuming the point of view) of a non-PA users.

The second phase of the experiment aimed to capture the perception that companies and citizens (non-PA users) had of the platform and the level of trust they had towards the PA. In particular, they were asked to provide information on the degree of completeness and comprehensibility of explanatory materials provided during the training sessions and to express a confidence rating, by stating whether they believed or not that the VPP was actually able to protect their personal data. To perform the experiment a complete and fully functional version of the VPP was deployed and users were free to set up their own privacy needs and preferences autonomously. Subjects used a fictitious scenario, yet inspired by the real model already tested in the first phase. Users' feedback to the questionnaire was gathered anonymously and then published on CKAN, a data management system that makes data accessible (i.e., open and available for everyone) to national and regional governments, companies and organizations.

Questionnaires

The questionnaires where structured as it follows:

1. receiving personal information (what do you do? what is your occupation? how are you involved in your organization? etc.),
2. trying to know, through a scoring system (from 1 to 5), the individual ratings or reactions to specific issues, for example the usability of the VPP, the reliability of PLAs, etc., in order to improve the setting of both objectives and hypotheses;
3. then questions became more specific, the participants were asked for example: "Do you think that the proposed questions cover adequately your privacy preferences?";
4. finally questions were formulated in a textual form, in order to investigate idiosyncrasies and exceptions, that could be useful to draw conclusions or hypothesis.

At the end of the VPP demo, users filled-in the questionnaire, in order to gather feedback on their personal satisfaction on the VPP.

4.2   Results

The empirical experiment conducted by MiSE consisted of a set of tests (*trials*), where each test, was a combination of treatments, subjects and objects. We should not confuse it, however, with ordinary statistical tests, since "experimental errors" are, in our case, primarily used to help us understand if the results are reliable and consistent with the goals we want to demonstrate [18].

Assuming that: (i) each test can be analyzed as a *"treatment"* (e.g., values that the different elements can take during an experiment); (ii) each treatment is applied to a combination of objects and subjects; (iii) *objects* can be seen as "topics" (specifically: the Web Framework, the Desktop Tools, participants' general confidence in the VPP, etc.); (iv) *subjects* can be identified as employees, operators, users, etc. (in our case, the administrative and technical staff of the Administration); (v) the different expertise of the staff (for example, IT operators, developers, project managers, users, etc.) and the different contexts (no matter how real or simulated) can be analyzed as if they were *"factors"*, that is to say "variables" that may differently influence the experiment; all considered, we can conclude that, in this experiment, we deal with a scheme that corresponds to a *multifactorial design*, as shown in Table 5 , with a *"stratified random sampling"* and a population divided into multiple groups (*strata*), whose distribution is well known and, at the same time, randomly selected. Moreover, the selection of subjects was made according to a *quota* and a *convenience* (the nearest and most convenient subjects, in order to demonstrate that the introduction of the VPP into CIPAQ was actually advantageous), a choice that probably don't match randomization techniques, but can help, however, the general purposes of the experiment and the balancing of methods.

Subjects Characterization
Subjects involved in the trials were selected considering the size of systems targeted by VisiOn, i.e., large and heterogeneous public administration systems.

Table 5. *Multifactorial design*

Factor A: Contexts							
Treatment A1: Simulated				Treatment A2: Real			
Factor B: Expertise				Factor B: Expertise			
Treatment B1': Subjects: IT Operators		Treatment B2': Subjects: Staff		Treatment B1": Subjects: IT Operators		Treatment B2": Subjects: Staff	
Treatment C: *on Topics*		Treatment C: *on Topics*		Treatment C: *on Topics*		Treatment C: *on Topics*	
Treatment C1': Objects: Desktop Tools	Treatment C2': Objects: Web Framework	Treatment C1': Objects: Desktop Tools	Treatment C2': Objects: Web Framework	Treatment C3': Objects Desktop Tools	Treatment C3': Objects: Web Framework	Treatment C4': Objects: Desktop Tools	Treatment C4': Objects: Web Framework

As a result, all possible combinations of subjects were included, in order to adapt them to the in-built characteristics of the experiment, as it follows.

- PA users (employees, IT operators) vs. non-PA users (citizens, companies)
- a specific case study (CIPAQ) vs. a general model (VisiOn)
- a desktop environment (the tools) vs. an on-line environment (the surveys)
- a simulated framework vs. a real context (MiSE's online services)

In addition, we tried to avoid any risk that could arise from dividing the empirical experiment into two different phases. Subjects were gradually prepared for surveys, through presentation meetings and training classes. Since the experiment consisted of a series of tests and treatments, the tests were planned in order to reach the largest number of population *samples*, considering either specific groups or individuals and asking them to play different roles.

The selection of voluntary participants, in such a wide range of professional roles and qualifications, reflected indeed very well the objectives of MiSE. MiSE expected in fact to broaden the range of feedback on the platform, not only in terms of quantity, but also in terms of quality and accuracy of analysis. Subjects engaged for the experiment were:

- 16 subjects to simulate a total number of 86 companies;
- 6 subjects among the technical staff to provide feedback on the VPP
- 6 subjects among users of CKAN

In total, 28 subjects were used for anonymous surveys.

Hypotheses Evaluation

In this section we analyze data collected during the experiment, in order to prove, or disprove, the hypotheses we formulated, which consisted in: (i) a high ease of usage of the platform; (ii) a high reliability of the VPP; (iii) and high users' trust in it. In other words, the main hypothesis was to demonstrate that the PLA was realistic enough and, to do this, it was primarily assessed to be tested by technical users and, therefore, by administrative ones, who could better make sense of data and verify whether they could be published or not by law. For that reason, the hypotheses were articulated up to foresee different phases and trials: the PLA needed to be set in a way that everybody could aspire to use, both PA and non-PA users. The analysis was based both on a quantitative and a qualitative approach, in order to acquire information and emerging elements that could meet the real scope of the investigation. Furthermore, the results were aggregated according to different type of users, distinguishing them into two main groups: internal users, on one side, and external stakeholders, on the other side.

Data were collected with questionnaires and with open questions and interviews. The former allowed a quantitative analysis of data retrieved, while with the latter we performed a qualitative analysis.

Qualitative Results

This section reports the feedback expressed by subjects during interviews. We collected the most significant and frequent feedback on the matter.

For what concerns PA users, some of them were not able to immediately understand how their data could have an intrinsic economic value, as shown by "visualization of the *economic value of data*", and this was a major cause of confusion for many.

The feedback from non-PA users was largely positive. Since their access to the Desktop Framework was limited and less frequent, they had little to do with the technical terminology used during the modeling phase and thus they appeared less confused than the others. Therefore, most of their improvement requests were concentrated on the "ease of use" and "accessibility"; for example, many users asked for an easier Italian translation of the Web Framework, less approximate and incomplete. Others called for a clearer distinction between the web components provided by the VPP (ViTo) and the practical demonstrations' system provided by MiSE, since the boundary between the two different contexts was not very clear and seemed often to easily overlap. Still, one of the most shared requests concerned the user interface, which was considered a little incoherent. Some web pages, in fact, especially the Economic Value view, were not properly displayed on some browsers, maybe because some tests of Web Framework were occasionally performed on small screens, as tablets or smartphones.

Quantitative Results

In total 261 subjects participated to the tests. 10 in the first phase, and 251 in the second phase.

The first questionnaire, i.e., the *PA Questionnaire*, was filled at the end of the first phase. Participants were chosen from the administrative and technical staff of the Administration and had different expertise in various fields of application of the Ministry. Each participant had to complete 5 tests, in a simulated environment: that means they had to play the role of 5 different companies, filling out different parameters. In particular, they had to answer questions related to the Desktop Tools, the Web Framework and their general confidence in the ability of the VPP to fulfill privacy issues.

Users were suggested, each time they changed the PLA, to fill out a new evaluation. Tracking every variation in users' opinion, while answering the questions, was not possible since we preserved anonymity of subjects. This prevented a more accurate analysis of changes and occurrences in progress. The amount of PLAs was greater than the number of participants, since users had to use fictitious personal data, the only way they could check their preferences inside the VPP was by generating a new PLA.

The second questionnaire was compiled after the second phase. It was distributed to all subjects that played the role of non-PA users and actually used the CIPAQ system with the VPP.

Analysis: PA Users

Important deductions can be drawn observing the results of the PA questionnaires shown in Table 6. The in the first question, *what type of user are you?*, 60% of users replied to be technical employees, while only 40% answered to be administrative employees. Such question is not represented in the table since it has a completely different set of answers. The results of all other questions are represented in the table.

Practically, Table 6 includes the percentages of the answers. For the complete set of answers, please refer to [1].

All participants (100%) claimed to find the VisiOn platform operational and accessible, while, as regards the documentation on the Desktop Framework (question 4), the answers were divided into two groups, the first, about 60%, was pretty satisfied with the documentation, finding it very useful and comprehensive, while the second, about 40%, was less satisfied, believing that it was useful enough, but not fully comprehensive. This makes us assume that the first group was probably composed of technical employees, while most of the second was composed of administrative employees, as the percentages are very similar to those recruited for the first question and are symptomatic of a significant involvement of both the groups: in fact, none of the respondents believed the documentation to be *"not useful at all"*. Again, at the question *how easy is to use the desktop framework?*, the answers revealed an identical percentage distribution, even if in this case the participants were asked to express a score from 1 to 5. Most of the participants declared that the tools were easy to use (question 4: *how easy is to use the desktop framework?*), but the majority of them believed that a technical training or a specific know-how was necessary to achieve this objective (question 13: *Are technical skills and competences necessary to use the tools of the platform?*). Once achieved this specific know-how, they would have modelled a socio-technical scenario, probably in a reasonable lapse of time (question 14: *Do you think that the result obtained is proportional at the effort spent for modeling?*). The platform was occasionally unstable (question 10, 11, 12), but this did not affect the ability to complete the assigned tasks.

Table 6. PA user questionnaire and results

ID	Questions	Strongly agree - Yes	Agree	Neutral	Disagree	Strongly disagree - No
2	Is the Vision platform operational and accessible?	100				0
3	Is the documentation on the desktop framework comprehensive and useful?	60	40	0	0	0
4	How easy is to use the desktop framework?	0	0	60	40	0
5	Is the desktop framework a convenient and comprehensive model to define the privacy policy?	0	0	30	40	30
7	How quickly were you able to model your scenario using the Vision platform?	10	60		30	0
8	How do you rate the VISION platform	0	0	40	60	0
10	Did you experience software freezes while using the platform?	10		90		0
11	Were you able to generate reports and export data correctly?	60		40		0
12	Is the platform stable and does it exhibit a deterministic behavior?	80				20
13	Were technical skills and competences necessary to use the tools of the platform?	20	70		10	0
14	Do you think that the result obtained is proportional at the effort spent for modeling?	30	70		0	0
15	How easy is to use the web framework?	0	20	0	40	40
16	Was it easy to create a questionnaire for end users?	40		60		0
17	Is the interface of the web platform user- friendly and easily navigable?	10	50	40	0	0

Questions 6 and 9 and 18 are not reported in the table, since they are open questions.

In particular, answers to question 6 (*explain briefly what were the gaps and weaknesses of the platform, if any*), clearly demonstrate doubts and uncertainties about the usability and comprehensibility of the platform, especially with regards to the tools and the user interface. Some subjects found it more difficult to understand than others, who, on the contrary, had already learned some basic concepts about the platform, having modelled and trained socio-technical scenarios (for example, IT workers). Other answers suggest perhaps a certain instability of the tools or a presence of bugs, even if many of the issues were immediately solved through the installation of updates and later builds. Indeed, many of the supposed bugs were caused by misunderstandings.

The free-text answers, instead, give us some important hints on the prevailing feelings of users towards the platform. As evidence of a common perception, answers to question 9 (*explain briefly the reasons for your rating*) demonstrate, in fact, that to deal proficiently with the VPP's tools, more than a single learning session was required and that in order to mitigate such difficulties, it would have been a good idea to improve the overall usability of the tools. In fact, some users, mostly administrative users, were accustomed to single, integrated applications, covering every aspect of a job or a given activity. So, for this kind of workers, it was a real disadvantage to deal with many small applications (the tools), not completely integrated and connected. However, once learned the basic techniques, everybody was able to complete his tasks anyway. Many of them also complained about the formal rigidity of this modeling approach, since in daily work, they said, laws change continuously and tasks must be frequently adapted to processes.

Answers to question 18 (*What would you improve in the interface of the web platform?*) are very significant, because they highlight a very common trend in today's society, in the sense that users nowadays are much more confident with modern web applications than with classic desktop software. Basically, they could easily understand what to do with the Web Framework, despite the uneasiness of the UI, while they claimed a complete lack of instructions for the Desktop Framework. They also suggested the provision of an online help system, but they didn't report, anyway, relevant malfunctions.

For the complete set of answers, please refer to [1].

Analysis: Web Users

As regards the non-PA Users, at the end of the trial session, the survey was filled out by a total of 251 people, generating overall 278 PLAs. Indeed, since a single user could edit his privacy preferences multiple times, he/she could also create more than one PLA. Table 7 (below) shows subjects' questions and answers, and it is structured as Table 6.

For example, question one (*What type of user are you?*) defined the type of subjects. The answer were: Citizen with 33,47%, Company with 47,01 % and Public Administration 19,52 %. The feedback on the experiment was widely positive (question 8). Even if, not all of the users were able to completely realize the potential of the platform, they seemed to be very engaged in a proper formulation of their own privacy issues, also because they were finally able to achieve this goal with an instrument that they could now usefully control on their own (question 5 and question 6). So, the quality of the material produced under the survey, suited their expectations (question 4), the model generated during the trials largely met their privacy needs (question 3) and, aided by this new know-how, they also were able to design their privacy needs without effort (question 7 and question 9). At the end of the trial, two out of three participants could better understand the "value of their data" (question 10).

Table 7. Web user questionnaire and results

ID	Questions	Strongly agree /Yes/1	Agree/2	Neither agree or disagree/3	Disagree/4	Strongly disagree/No/5
2	How clear was the information given?	59,76		35,06		05,18
3	Do you think that the proposed questions cover adequately your privacy preferences?	29,08	36,65	21,91	10,36	1,99
4	How clear are the questions of the presented questionnaire?	30,68	42,63	20,32	4,78	1,59
5	Are you satisfied with this initiative by MISE?	40,64	50,2	4,38	3,98	0,80
6	Do you think that the platform can be a valuable support to improve the handling of data and privacy by MISE?	93,23				6,77
7	How friendly and simple is the user interface?	31,47	40,24	18,33	8,37	1,59
8	Does this initiative increase your confidence in MISE?	84,06				15,94
9	Is monitoring and controlling your privacy preferences simple and intuitive?	82,07				17,93
10	It is easy to understand the economic value of your data?	61,35				38,65

Hypotheses Evaluation

The investigation (*cluster analysis*) was repeated in different ways for different groups of users, in order to intercept feasible trends or symptomatic differences between participants, i.e. citizens, companies and PA users (samples), with the purpose to find, through an in-depth analysis, patterns and keys to interpretation, that could help us to draw deductions and thus confirm our hypotheses.

Table 8 shows how the hypotheses were evaluated and whether they were confirmed or not by the data collected during the experiment.

4.3   Threats to Validity

We analyzed the threats of validity following the guidelines defined by Wohlin et al. in [18]. For what concerns this empirical experiment, it was not necessary to draw more general conclusions, in order to attain a *general validity*, since the experiment was conducted within the boundaries of public administration

Table 8. *Hypotheses evaluation*

Hypothesis	Result
Collect feedback on users' privacy expectations	**Confirmed**: this goal was widely achieved, users' involvement in privacy and security issues was very high and answers were balanced and promptly provided.
Value the ease of use of the platform	**Confirmed**: many of the participants stated that the VPP was easy and intuitive; so the idea of introducing the VPP into our administration was useful and totally in line with our expectations.
Estimate the potential and the reliability of the VPP	**Confirmed**: despite a not easy integration of the VPP into our IT systems and infrastructures, it showed great potential and reliability, both from a technical point of view and an operational point of view.
Rate the users' trust in its capabilities	**Confirmed**: users' trust in the VPP increased day by day, from session to session, as they could see in practice how it really worked in data protection and privacy enforcement

(MiSE) and thus designed to answer the questions that could satisfy specifically the needs and the institutional goals of this organization in particular. In other words, it was sufficient to achieve only an *"adequate validity"*, within the strict scope of the organization itself and not beyond.

In fact, adequate validity refers, more precisely, to a validity which is planned and pursued to meet exclusively the *population of interest*, that is the population from which the investigation sample is collected. So, if we say that the results of MiSE surveys have an adequate validity, we mean that they are suitable for MiSE, thus they can be generalized and applied, on a smaller scale, to all the processes and applications and contexts currently running within its organization.

Of course, talking about CIPAQ, the validity is adequate for CIPAQ, but can't be generalized to PA, on a larger scale. Nevertheless, we can extent it, by replicating and applying it to other similar structures and processes, always bearing in mind both the scale and context of the operation we are going to do. Now, we can also try to analyze the experiment, by intercepting both weaknesses and critical issues that normally may produce *threats* to the validity of the experiment, during the learning sessions as well as during the execution of the questionnaires.

From the point of a statistical relationship between the treatment and the outcome, we can surely say that most of the answers provided by the participants were in line with most of the questions formulated in the planning phase of the experiment, such as we can perceive through the qualitative analysis of the questionnaires. In fact, the choice of the questionnaires, tests and samples provided during the trials was sufficiently articulated and balanced, thus allowing to draw coherent conclusions about the scope and the trustworthiness of the VPP. The experiment results revealed the need to manage both administrative and IT processes under an increased awareness of data protection and privacy needs, was indubitable. In a broad sense, while both technical and administrative users revealed an adequate understanding of the theoretical environment and of the basic concepts underlying the tools, the administrative ones found it more difficult to apply it to a formal model, as expected by the tools. Also, many of them didn't possess an in-depth knowledge of English and, since the Desktop Framework (instructions plus user interface) was provided in English, their involvement became difficult.

We considered the following threats for what concerns *internal validity*:

1. different treatments were applied to the same object (the VPP), at different times (first phase and second phase), with different subjects (PA users vs. Web users), under different circumstances, and it was noticed that subjects reacted differently, depending on whether they were examined during the training phase, in which they had not yet tested the functionalities of the framework, or during a later stage, in which they had already tested it, being thus more acquainted with its real qualities; in the first case, they could act a bit confused, in the second, on the contrary, they could appear either tired and bored or enthusiastic and involved;

2. the *instrumentation* used to perform the experiment, such as documents, presentations, webinars, data collection forms, etc., was well designed, therefore, only a few participants did not understand the meaning of certain submissions (such as the "economic value of your data");

3. since subjects were classified into two main experimental groups (PA users and non-PA users), there was a real risk depending on how the subjects were selected, especially because one of the two groups (PA users) were asked to perform the role on non-PA users (for example, the role of companies, in a simulated environment). This might have negatively influenced the results, since the PA users were less motivated than companies to provide truthful answers. Maybe, we can hypothesize that the selected group was not fully representative for the designated population (the companies);

4. we also considered social cohesion inside the groups, since two different treatments were applied at different stages of the experiment. The old system without the VPP was compared to the new system with the VPP, and of course, this might have influenced the participants to prefer the second to the first, providing perhaps not properly objective or neutral answers. Besides, some participants might have learned about the treatment from the previous group of participants, trying to imitate both the behavior and the responses, even if this didn't cause in the groups any attitude of "compensatory rivalry", since all groups were compensated and treated in exactly the same way. On the other hand, we detected some limited cases of demoralization among administrative operators, due to a lacking knowledge of IT issues.

As for *"construct validity"*, the entire conceptual contribution from MiSE was predetermined, as a consequence of its commitment to the project. Therefore, it was assigned and entirely allocated into the theoretical system of the project itself, which was developed, as already mentioned, in a very complex way, involving numerous partners and components, through different stages and packages. Nevertheless, since the theoretical assumptions of the project were applied also to a smaller level, it is possible that some interactions, in terms of testing and treatment, may have escaped the control of MiSE, and surely the way the experiment was adapted to the needs of MiSE or even the way the "modeling tools" were used to redesign such internal services as the CIPAQ, may present some inappropriate deviations or forced adjustments, to suite the general coherence of the model, but basically *"construct validity"* was regularly respected. Finally, with regards to the *"external validity"* of the experiment, specifically the ability to generalize the results of the empirical experiment to a real industrial practice, surely the experiment was conducted, on some occasions, under unfavorable circumstances, for instance after a crash or a malfunctioning, so users tended to answer negatively or frustrated, and this, of course, gave no boost to the experiment, neither in direction of a further implementation of the project itself, nor in the direction of a new quality standard, like VPP is. But surely the most important threat to external validity was represented by the use of old-fashioned tools, like many outdated applications still in use, whose effect is simply devastating, in a perspective of industrial practice, and blocks the ordinary implementation of software.

4.4   Discussions on the Empirical Experiment

Subjects revealed a considerable estimation for the initiative, showing that the transparent management of administrative activities is a prerequisite of a larger involvement of citizens in the control of their own data, as well as the "main road" to raise a lasting relationship of trust between citizens, companies and the PA . Of course, it is difficult to assess whether the results of the experiment itself validate the initial expectations (*hypotheses*) or not. The most risky point of the whole process, which makes us fear for a low statistical value of the experiment, lies in the fact that much of the experiment itself was achieved through simulated scenarios into simulated contexts, with fictitious data and players, and this is an obvious threat to internal, external and construct validity, both of the hypotheses and the results. However, this was inevitably, because of the nature of the case study itself, CIPAQ is indeed a real production environment, hence data collected during business procedures can't be used outside CIPAQ itself and its purposes.

The VPP increased the awareness of possible issues related to privacy and security and how they can be solved through a careful analysis of administrative scenarios and an effective use of modeling tools. The "privacy by design" principle adopted by the VPP required to analyze security and privacy requirements within administrative processes and IT systems:

- a socio-technical perspective (Socio Technical Security-Tool (STS-Tool) [5]), was used to define interactions between actors and contexts;
- a procedural perspective (Secure Business Process Modelling Notation 2.0 (SecBPMN2) [15]), was used to define business processes improved with security information;
- a trust perspective (JTrust [12,13]), was adopted to define institutional relationships between MiSE, other PAs , citizens, companies and stakeholders in terms of mutual confidence;
- a security perspective (SecTro2 [10]), was used to define potential threats to data and privacy issues and to avoid attacks or mitigate risks.

All these steps were carried out by MiSE with the awareness and the intent to introduce PLA into its administrative systems. The following difficulties were encountered while executing the empirical experiment:

- the institutional role of the MiSE can probably be considered as the first reason why privacy and security policies were in fact so restrictive and sensitive data couldn't be managed for testing purpose;
- most of our IT services were "outsourced", so, it was difficult to integrate third-party systems, such as the VPP, into our internal IT systems, since only a small percentage of IT coperators was actually internal and most of the services were not fully managed by MiSE or probably they were managed only at a staff level;
- moreover, an HTTP proxy, prohibited any access to the outside, thus isolating the internal network itself; this was especially the case of MANE (Media Network Aware Element), used in the VPP to capture and analyze the network traffic by reading the data packets' payload, through a technology called Deep Packet Inspection (DPI), which suggests that network flows are effectively inspected and information is extracted from higher layers of packet data (up to application layer); this approach was unfortunately not applicable to our internal security policies, both the Internal Domain and the Office Information Systems.

Since the VPP provides end users with the opportunity to clearly and intuitively express their own privacy preferences, by understanding the potential threats to privacy as well as the subtle aspects related to trust, the overall awareness of the economic value of data is expected to grow. On the other hand, from the point of view of the PA, the platform will allow a more exact perception of end users' expectations and of how their privacy needs, according to the PLA, should be considered and respected. Thanks to the VisiOn platform, public administrations can now access useful indicators and tools to improve transparency and increase citizens' confidence in administrative processes.

Thanks to open and dynamic online services such as Cloud Computing, Big Data and the Internet of Things, the exchange of information is nowadays simple and fast, with an availability of 24 h a day and seven days a week. On the contrary, especially among private citizens, there is a certain reluctance to use these services, probably due to a perceived loss of control over data and technologies. This scenario becomes even more complex when you enter the Public Administration area, which manages data of millions of citizens, who, moreover, are not free to deny access to their data, as they normally do with commercial companies, since public institutions are authorized by law to acquire personal data from citizens. For this reason, improving services, efficiency and the overall functioning of Public Administration with a proper data management is a matter of strategic and global interest. Public administrations should provide secure and reliable data management services, be transparent and then report them to citizens.

Altogether, the VPP has proven to be a powerful and valuable way to increase internal knowledge of administrative processes and to provide end users with an effective tool for tracking their data. All the experiences made during the experimentation have further confirmed this impression, with positive consequences in terms of *"governance"*, which is fundamental to perform important tasks in the domain of privacy and security. Perhaps this is one of the main reasons why MiSE firmly believes that the VPP is a valid market solution, which can easily be integrated in existing IT systems and online services, as an added value for citizens and the whole business market.

5   Conclusions

This chapter described three empirical experiments in three very different domains. The choice of different domains has proved to be valid since each company received heterogeneous feedback from the subjects involved. The outcome of the empirical experiments is clear: the VPP has a lot of potential and can be used in order to increase the privacy of PA and the awareness of citizens on privacy issues, by giving them the possibility to configure their privacy preferences. VPP provides an easy to use tool to citizens for managing their privacy preferences and a complete software to manage sensitive data of citizens, for the PA employees. The VPP has also the potentiality to be installed and executed in the cloud, however, this can be a tempting option for private companies (such as DAEM) while it cannot be feasible for PA (such as MiSE). The PLA was generally appreciated by the subjects and succeed in helping to increase the trust of the citizens in the platform and, consequently, in the PA.

The integration of VPP in existing software took most of the resources of the companies. The VPP is a complete yet not mature software, therefore, components were tailored for the specific scenarios and some were only partially integrated. Nevertheless, the contribution of this evaluation of the VPP is priceless because provided feedback on the platform as a whole and allowed the consortium to focus on the parts with most negative feedback, i.e., the interface and integration of the Desktop components.

Acronyms

GDPR	General Data Protection Regulation
PA	Public Administration
EU	European Union
ICT	Information and Communication Technologies
PLA	Privacy Level Agreement
VPP	VisiOn Privacy Platform
C	Citizen
SecBPMN2	Secure Business Process Modelling Notation 2.0
DPI	Deep Packet Inspection
ATA	American Telemedicine Association's
EHR	Electronic Health Record
OPBG	Ospedale Pediatrico Bambino Gesu'
HIUNJ	Hospital Infantil Universitario Niño Jesus
MACS	Municipality of Athens Computer System
IT	Information Technology
STS-Tool	Socio Technical Security-Tool
CoA	City of Athens
GQM	Goal Question Metric
CIPAQ	"Credito d'Imposta Per l'Assunzione di personale Qualificato", transl.: "Tax credits for hiring skilled personnel"

References

1. VSN-RP-145 D5.2 VisiOn Pilots Report-final. Technical report VisiOn (2017)
2. Yttri, Arora, Nilsen: Privacy and security in mobile health (mHealth) research. Alcohol Res. **36**(1) (2014)
3. ATA. Purpose of the TeleICU/Acute Care SIG Committee. http://www.americantelemed.org/main/membership/ata-members/ata-sigs/teleicu-sig. Last visit September 2018
4. Brous: Legal considerations in telehealth and telemedicine. Am. J. Nurs. **116**(9) (2016)
5. Dalpiaz, F., Paja, E., Giorgini, P.: Security Requirements Engineering: Designing Secure Socio-Technical Systems (2015). To appear
6. Rowbotham, McConnell, Ashley, Grady, Cummings, Kang: Informed consent. New Engl. J. Med. **376** (2017)
7. Hale, Kvedar: Privacy and security concerns in telehealth. AMA J. Ethics **16**(12) (2014)
8. Hall, McGrow: For telehealth to succeed, privacy and security risks must be identified and addressed. Health Aff. **33**(2) (2014)
9. Locatis, Liu, Zhang, Ackerman: Cloud and traditional videoconferencing technology for telemedicine and distance learning. Telemed. J. E Health **21**(5) (2015)
10. Mouratidis, H., Giorgini, P.: Secure tropos: a securityoriented extension of the tropos methodology. Int. J. Software Eng. Knowl. Eng. **17**(02), 285–309 (2007)
11. The European Parliament and the Council of the European Union. REGULATION (EU) 2016/679 OF THE EUROPEAN PARLIAMENT AND OF THE COUNCIL (2016). http://ec.europa.eu/justice/data-protection/reform/files/regulation_oj_en.pdf

12. Pavlidis, M., et al.: Dealing with trust and control: a meta-model for trustworthy information systems development. In: 2012 Sixth International Conference on Research Challenges in Information Science (RCIS), pp. 1–9. IEEE (2012)
13. Pavlidis, M., et al.: Modeling trust relationships for developing trustworthy information systems. International Journal of Information System Modeling and Design (IJISMD) **5**(1), 25–48 (2014)
14. Raposo: Telemedicine: the legal framework (or the lack of it) in Europe. GMS Health Technol. Assess. **12** (2016)
15. Salnitri, M., Paja, E., Giorgini, P.: Maintaining secure business processes in light of socio-technical systems' evolution. In: Proceeding of Model-Driven Requirement Engineering (MoDRE) Workshop, IEEE International, pp. 155–164. IEEE (2016)
16. Salnitri, M., et al.: Visual Privacy Management: Design and Applications of a Privacy-Enabling Platform-Evaluation Results (2020). https://doi.org/10.17632/vs8m5xvbm9.1
17. Basili, V., Trendowicz, A., et al.: Aligning Organizations Through Measurement
18. Wohlin, C., et al.: Experimentation in Software Engineering. Springer, Heidelberg (2012)
19. Host, Wohlin, Regnell: Experimentation in Software Engineering. Springer, Heidelberg (2012)

Correction to: Visual Privacy Management

Mattia Salnitri⑩, Jan Jürjens⑩, Haralambos Mouratidis⑩,
Loredana Mancini⑩, and Paolo Giorgini⑩

Correction to:
M. Salnitri et al. (Eds.): *Visual Privacy Management,*
LNCS 12030, https://doi.org/10.1007/978-3-030-59944-7

In the original version of this book, the name of the second editor was not correct. This has now been rectified.

The updated version of the book can be found at
https://doi.org/10.1007/978-3-030-59944-7

Author Index

Printed in the United States
By Bookmasters